EXPORT NOW

FIVE KEYS TO ENTERING NEW MARKETS

EXPORT NOW

FIVE KEYS TO ENTERING NEW MARKETS

FRANK LAVIN & PETER COHAN

FOREWORD BY FORMER U.S. SECRETARY OF COMMERCE GARY LOCKE

WILEY

John Wiley & Sons, (Asia) Pte. Ltd.

Copyright © 2011 by John Wiley & Sons (Asia) Pte. Ltd.
Published in 2011 by John Wiley & Sons (Asia) Pte. Ltd.
1 Fusionopolis Walk, #07–01 Solaris, South Tower Singapore 138628

Other Wiley Editorial Offices

John Wiley & Sons, 111 River Street, Hoboken, NJ 07030, USA

John Wiley & Sons, The Atrium, Southern Gate, Chichester, West Sussex, P019 8SQ, United Kingdom

John Wiley & Sons (Canada) Ltd., 5353 Dundas Street West, Suite 400, Toronto, Ontario, M9B 6HB, Canada

John Wiley & Sons Australia Ltd, 42 McDougall Street, Milton, Queensland 4064, Australia

Wiley-VCH, Boschstrasse 12, D-69469 Weinheim, Germany

Library of Congress Cataloging-in-Publication Data

ISBN 978-0-470-82816-8 (Hardback)
ISBN 978-0-470-82818-2 (ePDF)
ISBN 978-0-470-82817-5 (eMobi)
ISBN 978-0-470-82819-9 (ePub)

Typeset in 11.5/14.5 Sabon Roman by MPS Limited, a Macmillan Company
Printed in Singapore by Markono Print Media Pte Ltd

CONTENTS

FOREWORD

Globalization means that it has never been easier for your company to enter new markets. Large or small, your company is a part of the global economy today more than ever before. You might find a customer in Korea or Peru. You might find a competitor in France or China. You might license your technology in Mexico and find a distributor in Malaysia. You might enter into a joint venture in Brazil and find an investor in Great Britain who wants you to double your business.

As the Governor of Washington state—the nation's most trade-dependent state—from 1996 to 2004, I helped open doors for Washington state businesses worldwide. In addition to leading ten productive trade missions to Asia, Mexico, and Europe, I focused on strengthening economic ties between China and Washington state.

This experience gave me a practitioner's view of the challenges companies face when they enter new markets—as well as the necessity of doing so. We occasionally stumbled as we ventured abroad; not every market entry was easy or simple. But companies learned, we adapted, and we were willing to modify our approach as we went along. During my time as Governor, we more than doubled the state's exports to China, to over $5 billion per year.

When President Obama asked me to serve as Secretary of Commerce, I saw that companies nationwide were grappling with the same questions and challenges as companies in my own state, but often with fewer resources and even less international experience. I found the same pattern again and again: terrific companies, great products and people, but limited understanding of what it took to compete and win internationally. But I have learned what is possible. Through the National Export Initiative announced in 2010 by President Obama, I am confident we can double U.S. exports and support millions of jobs.

To help achieve the National Export Initiative goals, Frank Lavin (who formerly served as Under Secretary for International Trade at the Commerce Department) and Peter Cohan have produced this timely and useful book. The authors lead you expertly and methodically through the process of exporting goods and services. You will find an effective approach to export planning, including practical tools that give you what many U.S. exporters lack: a plan for entering new markets and finding new buyers. The real-world case studies are filled with examples of how to increase the chances of success and reduce the chances of failure. Today, exporting is easier than ever, and more companies—especially smaller ones—are doing it. But success requires preparation, and this book helps ensure that you prepare thoughtfully and strategically.

Finally, for the American readers of this book, the Department of Commerce's International Trade Administration is ready to go to work for you as you start to plan your approach to exporting or seek to enter additional country markets. Please visit www.export.gov to find the U.S. Export Assistance Center near you.

I am proud to lead a team of highly capable trade professionals who are dedicated to helping U.S. companies export successfully. Give them a call today.

Gary Locke
Former U.S. Secretary of Commerce

ACKNOWLEDGMENTS

We are deeply grateful for the help of many people during the creation of this book. Richard Edelman, Robert Rehg, Audrey Lavin, Maud Lavin, Abby Lavin, Ann Lavin, Robin Cohan, and Dan Kadison provided support, valuable advice, or help with the copy editing.

Francisco Sanchez, Michelle O'Neill, Courtney Gregoire, Alex Feldman, Izzy Hernandez, Matt Englehardt, Charley Skuba, David Bohigian, Susan Dugan, R.J. Donovan, Susan Lusi, and Andrew Wylegala offered useful feedback on our drafts, helped shape the approach that we used in the book, and worked to ensure that our efforts would reinforce the Department of Commerce's own efforts.

Chihuahua Cattle & Cotton's Gary Stowe, WATG's Howard Wolff, AHAVA's Yacov Ellis, Celeno's Gilad Rozen, BrewDog's James Watt, and GP Graders' Stuart Payne offered highly useful personal insights into their companies' export strategies.

We are very grateful to Nick Wallwork, Jules Yap, Janis Soo, and Kristi Hein of John Wiley Asia, who brought this project from idea to finished product.

Henry Winter, Doug Lavin, Robert Roche, Bob Zulkoski, and Michael Jemal of Export Now offered valuable support for our promotion of the book—including lending their company name to the book's title.

PART ONE

WHY AND WHAT:
SETTING YOUR EXPORT GOALS

Chapter One

WHERE'S THE WORLD GOING?

Former Secretary of Commerce Gary Locke pointed out that "it has never been easier for your company to enter new markets." Indeed, we can sum up the reason for this book—and the reason you need to read it—in one sentence: it has never been easier for a foreign competitor to enter your market, and it has never been easier for you to enter a foreign market. To put it more urgently: the world is not standing still. There is enormous business risk if *you* try to stand still.

Some people are in denial regarding this core truth, even as they lose market share to foreign competition. Others understand the reality but are paralyzed by the seeming complexity of entering new markets. Let's face it, if you have been building a successful small business in your home market over the past ten or twenty years, you may think yourself as capable of successfully tackling a foreign market as you are of, well, flying a spaceship. You may think that *other* people—those with years of training—might well be able to export, but it is not realistic to expect this of the average businessperson.

Fortunately, just about everyone can achieve some level of success in a foreign market—regardless of how much export experience they have to begin with. Those who achieve their business goals understand that every activity involves a degree of uncertainty, even in a home market. Thus tackling a new market may not be much different from expanding capacity at home, launching a new product, or adding a new distribution hub. All of these business tasks involve a bit of a journey and require a bit of wherewithal to prevail. Planning and studying are part of this journey. International business is no different.

There's more to this book, of course, than an elaboration of the core point of ease of entry into foreign markets, but it is not a bad place to start. Businesses face a starkly different environment than they did even a few decades ago—due to a confluence of economic, political, and technological changes that we explore in this chapter.

Broadly speaking, this book focuses on where you are going, or where your business is going. The world is moving faster and is more open. Businesses need to develop a trade strategy, regardless of whether they eventually go international. But before we focus specifically on you and your business, we want to devote this chapter to understanding what has happened to international trade in recent years and how that shapes the business environment. The pace of change in international business has accelerated dramatically within one generation, and many businesses that still have limited involvement in exporting need to take stock of these changes. So before we turn to the "how to" part of the book, let's first try to understand these changes.

Discussions of trade frequently lapse into jargon or take on a pessimistic tone. The gloom is understandable, as recent years have seen a series of challenging developments in trade policy. Headlines proclaim that the Doha Trade Round—the trade-negotiation round begun by the World Trade Organization (WTO) in 2001—is in trouble. The lapse of the U.S. president's Trade Promotion Authority—effectively killing future trade negotiations—is cheered in Congress. Protectionist pressures mount in major economies such as the United States, the European Union (EU), and China. Trade liberalization seems to be on a slow path. Meanwhile, the number of formal trade actions and antidumping and countervailing duty cases hits record highs.[1]

These recent developments highlight the central economic paradox of our era: although international trade has never been more important to the world economy, political support for trade seems to be at a historical weak point. To take one example, a recent poll shows that 68 percent of the U.S. public believes that "trade restrictions are necessary to protect domestic industries," and only 24 percent support free trade.[2] If trade is so good for us, why does it not enjoy broader support?

Trade's High Benefits and Low Support

First, let us revisit the good news. Even in the midst of a painful global economic recession, trade continued to do very well. In 2009, global trade was near its historic peak, in both dollar terms and as a percentage of gross domestic product (GDP). Let's look at some U.S. figures as a reference point. U.S. merchandise exports totaled US$1,278 billion in 2010, up 21 percent from 2009.[3] More companies than ever are competing and winning overseas. Every nine months the United States exports the equivalent of the entire economy of Brazil. The fourteen nations that have free trade agreements (FTAs) with the United States account for only 7 percent of all of its trading partners' GDP, yet they take in 42 percent of U.S. exports.[4] And, as illustrated in Figure 1.1, merchandise trade as a share of global GDP has risen from nearly 9 percent in 1960 to 160 percent in 2009.[5]

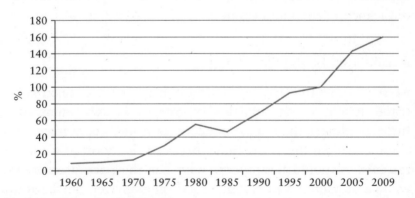

FIGURE 1.1   Merchandise Trade as a Percentage of World GDP (1960 to 2009)
Source: World Trade Organization, Peter S. Cohan & Associates analysis.

These FTAs help in another way: they help drive inward investment. When a foreign company invests in the United States, or Australia, or Singapore, it attains access not only to those markets, but also to the market of all their FTA partners. The U.S. FTA market in aggregate is almost six hundred million people; the Australian FTA market is a bit larger, as it includes ASEAN; and the Singapore FTA market is almost two billion, as it includes China. Free trade agreements work. The world is in the middle of a sustained export boom. The success of trade is real.[6]

But this also means that the world is in the middle of a sustained import boom as well, and there is a real basis for the criticism of trade policy. Particularly in a period of economic softness, there is a willingness to view trade as the enemy—as an agent of misery, not a spur to prosperity.

This disconnect between the benefits of trade and the support for it is perhaps due more to sociology than to economics. The rate of change in the modern economy outpaces most people's comfort level, so people project their various economic concerns—job insecurity, a perceived decline in manufacturing base, a sense of economic vulnerability—against trade.[7] A domestic political discussion on trade sometimes escalates into a general expression of economic unease or descends to political criticism of the incumbent administration.

Accelerated Economic Change

Merely presenting the bare facts concerning the negatives of trade deficits or the benefits of free trade agreements does little to address the unease concerning trade. Economics alone cannot explain the discrepancy between the boon of trade and the lack of political support. Why has the pace of economic change accelerated in recent years? The answer can be found in three developments that have collectively created a seismic shift in the world economy over several decades: three billion new customers, the death of distance, and the overthrow of trade barriers.

The emergence of **three billion new customers** reflects the transformation of the world economy brought about over the past three decades as China, and later India, moved to market economies. Consistent with this trend, and somewhat prompted by it, has been a move to market rationalism in much of Latin America, as well as the integration of Central Europe and much of the former Soviet Union into the world economy. This massive shift in economic behavior suggests not only three billion new customers, but also, perhaps, three billion new competitors—a more troubling, if inaccurate, prospect. In short, the economic population of this planet has effectively doubled in one generation.[8]

The **death of distance** refers to the rapid decline of geography as a business constraint.[9] Goods, people, and ideas move around the world rapidly and inexpensively. Business activities that once had to be undertaken at one locale can now be disaggregated and spread around the world. The advent of e-mail, the Internet, mobile phones, and webcams has led to a collapse in the cost of communication. The emergence of global express delivery, integrated logistics, containerized shipping, and discount air travel has led to a sharp reduction in transportation costs. Goods and ideas move around the world cheaper and faster than at any time in history. Many services, from accounting to design to customer relations, can be handled without regard to the location of the customer or the service provider. Mumbai is next door. Monterrey is your best customer. Shanghai sits next to you in class.

The **elimination of tariffs** refers to the cumulative impact of sixty years of reductions of trade barriers by the General Agreement on Tariffs and Trade (GATT) and World Trade Organization (WTO) along with the benefits of the over six hundred free trade agreements currently in place.[10] As shown in Figure 1.2, when the United States helped launch GATT in 1947, as one of the twenty-three founding members, the average U.S. tariff rate was 38.5 percent. Today the WTO has 153 members and the average U.S. tariff rate is less than 4 percent—a 90-percent reduction.

In sum, this seismic shift means that unparalleled prosperity goes hand in hand with unparalleled anxiety. The world is spinning faster.

The Business Impact

The economics of trade tell us this is all good news. But the business side can present a more mixed picture.

First, every company needs to think about exporting. It is no longer safe to remain content in your home market. Sooner or later, you are likely to face threats from foreign entrants. You need to find a way to take the offensive and enter new markets.

Second, this means a shift from vertical skills to horizontal skills. Most businesses exist in the vertical. They have a small set of core competencies, and they devote their business life to successful execution of that skill set. Now you have to develop horizontal skills. How can you evaluate a market you have never visited? How can you sell to someone you have never

---

GATT Membership 1947

Australia	Lebanon
Belgium	Luxembourg
Brazil	Netherlands
Burma	New Zealand
Canada	Norway
Ceylon	Pakistan
Chile	South Africa
China	Southern Rhodesia
Cuba	(now Zimbabwe)
Czechoslovakia	Syria
France	United Kingdom
India	United States of America

FIGURE 1.2   GATT Membership at Inception and as of 2011

WTO Membership 2011

Albania	The Gambia	Nigeria
Angola	Georgia	Norway
Antigua and Barbuda	Germany	Oman
Argentina	Ghana	Pakistan
Armenia	Greece	Panama
Australia	Grenada	Papua New Guinea
Austria	Guatemala	Paraguay
Bahrain	Guinea	Peru
Bangladesh	Guinea Bissau	Philippines
Barbados	Guyana	Poland
Belgium	Haiti	Portugal
Belize	Honduras	Qatar
Benin	Hong Kong, China	Romania
Bolivia	Hungary	Rwanda
Botswana	Iceland	Saint Kitts and Nevis
Brazil	India	Saint Lucia
Brunei Darussalam	Indonesia	Saint Vincent & the
Bulgaria	Ireland	Grenadines
Burkina Faso	Israel	Saudi Arabia
Burundi	Italy	Senegal
Cambodia	Jamaica	Sierra Leone
Cameroon	Japan	Singapore
Canada	Jordan	Slovak Republic
Cape Verde	Kenya	Slovenia
Central African Republic	Korea	Solomon Islands
Chad	Kuwait	South Africa
Chile	Kyrgyz Republic	Spain
China	Latvia	Sri Lanka
Colombia	Lesotho	Suriname
Congo	Liechtenstein	Swaziland
Costa Rica	Lithuania	Sweden
Côte d'Ivoire	Luxembourg	Switzerland
Croatia	Macao, China	Chinese Taipei
Cuba	Madagascar	Tanzania
Cyprus	Malawi	Thailand
Czech Republic	Malaysia	Togo
Democratic Republic of the Congo	Maldives	Tonga
Denmark	Mali	Trinidad and Tobago
Djibouti	Malta	Tunisia
Dominica	Mauritania	Turkey
Dominican Republic	Mauritius	Uganda
Ecuador	Mexico	Ukraine
Egypt	Moldova	United Arab Emirates
El Salvador	Mongolia	United Kingdom
Estonia	Morocco	United States of America
European Union (formerly	Mozambique	Uruguay
European Communities)	Myanmar	Venezuela
Fiji	Namibia	Vietnam
Finland	Nepal	Zambia
Former Yugoslav Republic of	Netherlands	Zimbabwe
Macedonia (FYROM)	New Zealand	
France	Nicaragua	
Gabon	Niger	

FIGURE 1.2 (*Continued*)
Source: World Trade Organization

met? How can you navigate government regulations in foreign countries?

Third, your business will need to develop a culture of flexibility and innovation. This does not mean that every day you will generate a new product, or that every new market will require a new approach. However, markets, customers, and opportunities differ, and a wise business knows how to take advantage of these differences.

Trade will create more winners than losers, but there are likely to be losers, including companies that cannot adjust to a more competitive environment, companies whose entire approach to trade is defensive, and companies that are unable to experiment. These companies run a higher risk of failure than their counterparts.

Every company has strengths and weaknesses, and because trade places these attributes in a broader market, we can say that trade brings into play a "magnification effect." It magnifies your company's strengths and weaknesses. If your company has a weak warehouse and distribution system selling in your domestic market, you can expect those weaknesses to be magnified when you start selling into foreign markets. On the other hand, if your company has a killer app technology product that dominates the sector in your home market, you could be well on your way to dominating that sector in new markets as well.

In this sense, the stratification that comes from trade is somewhat similar to the economic impact of the advent of a new technology. For example, not everyone benefits from the Internet, but it does confer economic benefits. High school graduates who cannot use the Internet will find themselves much less attractive to employers. The challenge of trade is similar to the challenge of a new technology: how can we shape the benefits to be as inclusive as possible? Trade and technology create many more winners than losers, but there is an asymmetry between good news and bad news. Factory closings tend to make the front page, but factory openings are more likely to be a note inside the business section. Additionally, human psychology ascribes importance to relative loss, apart from any absolute loss. So even if a group of workers receive real salary increases, they may have a sense of grievance if those increases have been outpaced by those of other workers.

A Trend or a Shift?

Interestingly, just as the political anxiety over trade seems to be peaking, the economic dislocation from trade may be abating. Astronomers tell us that a supernova burns the brightest as it moves toward collapse; we may have a similar sociopolitical phenomenon unfolding.

We must remember that the three major trends—three billion new customers, death of distance, and the elimination of tariffs—are perhaps more representative of a shift in the economic landscape than of an economic trend. In other words, once the economic adjustment to the improvements in logistics has been made, additional efficiencies are more marginal. Similarly, the early stages of China's integration into the international economy cause more of a jolt than the latter stages. And once tariffs have been cut 90 percent, there is not likely to be as much economic dislocation from the remaining 10 percent.

Recent trade statistics point to a rough equivalence in the growth of imports and exports. In 2010, total imports into the United States were up 22.6 percent and total exports from the United States were up 21 percent.[11] Admittedly, these imports are on a higher base, so the trade deficit itself continues to grow, but that rate of growth is tapering off. These numbers capture a world economy on the rebound after the 2008 financial turmoil, so the 2010 numbers probably outpace the longer-term trend. The point is that even though the three trends are somewhat permanent economic features, their effects are more similar to one-off phenomena.

It could take a generation of economic adjustment to fully understand these trends, but we are already seeing increasing economic anecdotes from China that the current high rates of economic growth are likely to attenuate. A growing body of literature discusses the decline in China's competitiveness due to rising wage rates, congested infrastructure, and constraints in its finance and legal systems.[12] To this are sometimes added costs of pollution, health care, demographic challenges of gender asymmetry and declining birth rates, as well as a changing tax policy.[13] China's economy should continue to perform strongly for the near term, and even if it slows down it should outperform the rate of growth in the United States. It should surprise no one over the next decade if the rate of growth in U.S. imports from China looks increasingly like the rate of growth in imports from other countries. In other words, as China's economy matures, its trade patterns will look increasingly similar to the patterns of other countries. This is not the beginning of the end for China's exports, which are driven by a mammoth and successful economy. But to paraphrase Churchill, it is, perhaps, the end of the beginning. The United States needs to stop devising trade policy by looking in the rearview mirror.

The foregoing analysis leads to an inescapable conclusion: in order to grow, many companies are going to need to sell their products into economies that are growing faster than the economy of their home country. The purpose of this book is to answer basic questions about such exporting: Why? What? How? and When?

How This Book Can Help Your Company Export

This book gives you the tools you need to compete and win in this new international business environment. Specifically, this book is designed to help you, a leader of a small-or medium-sized enterprise (SME), to enter foreign markets and generate meaningful sales growth there. We believe that the concepts, cases, methodologies, and checklists we present in this book—drawn from over thirty years' experience helping thousands of companies evaluate whether and how to expand into global markets, as well as from specific research conducted for this book—can boost your odds of export success.

To do this, we have organized the book into three broad parts. The first focuses on how you can decide on your export goals. The second and longest part develops methods for making the key strategic choices that will determine success. The final part is intended to help you make your export strategy happen.

Here's an outline of how each part addresses these challenges.

Part One. Why and What? includes two chapters intended to help you to (1) examine the broad trends in the world that will affect your thinking about potential opportunities and threats, and (2) take a look within to decide whether you have the drive and energy you'll need to overcome the inevitable obstacles you will encounter as you initiate an export strategy.

- **Chapter One. Where's the World Going?** provides an overview of key shifts in the way the economy works around the world and the kinds of threats and opportunities these shifts present.
- **Chapter Two. Where Are *You* Going?** gives you a glimpse of the kinds of challenges that companies face when they export and a sense of how you can decide whether you have the level of commitment needed to launch an export strategy. This chapter and the seven that follow each begin with a fictitious case study—drawn from real life— of a company's experience in launching an export venture and then consider lessons from real-life case studies that apply to the fictitious company's experience.

Part Two. How? includes five chapters aimed at helping you choose your export strategy. We recommend a sequence of go/no-go analyses. You will consider a series of five key questions—we call them the 5Cs. If you can answer "yes" to the first, then you proceed to the next question, and so on. If you answer "yes" to all five questions, then you can comfortably conclude that you have a robust export strategy.

- **Chapter Three. Country: Pick the Right One** suggests that you start off with an export strategy that does not require you to learn a totally different culture from the one with which you are already familiar. This chapter provides concepts, cases, a methodology, and a checklist to help you find such a country to kick off your export strategy. We believe that if you can succeed in culturally similar countries, you can always consider later moves to more challenging locales.

- **Chapter Four. Customers: How They Differ** argues that once you pick the country in which you'll launch your export strategy, you ought to focus on who your customers will be—these may be both distributors and product consumers—and what they will need from you. Like Chapter Three, this chapter provides tools to help you identify how the needs of customers in the new country differ from those in your home country and whether you can give those customers something better than what competitors offer. The critical point is that the customer preferences in the new market may not be the same as those in the old market. So meeting customer preferences requires an understanding of what differences there may be. If you can answer "yes" to this customer question, you can proceed to the next step in the analysis.

- **Chapter Five. Competitors: A Different Market** recommends that you study the competition in the new market. We also emphasize studying the competition as part of understanding a new market, meaning distribution, financing, regulations, and so on. We argue that you can gain important insights from studying competitors: determining whether you can occupy a unique market position that will be valuable to customers, and learning what capabilities those competitors are deploying to hold onto their market positions. But the first question that you need to answer is really the key—if you can offer a unique product that customers want to buy and that competitors will have a tough time copying, you can answer "yes" to the Competitor question and continue to the next.

- **Chapter Six. Capabilities: What You Need to Win** taps into the second part of the competitor analysis. This chapter helps you to identify the specific capabilities required to meet the needs of customers in the new country. These capabilities may be as simple as finding a reliable distributor or as complex as setting up manufacturing, distribution, supply, R&D, marketing, sales, and service capabilities in the new country or around the world. If you conclude that you have these capabilities—or can partner to get them—you can answer "yes" to the capabilities question.
- **Chapter Seven. Capability Gap: How to Close It** keys off of this last point. We expect that for most SMEs, there is a good chance that they will need to partner to close the capability gap. This could mean that the SME needs to find a reliable distributor in that country who can sell, finance, and service its product. Or the SME could find that it needs a series of partners for the different capabilities required to compete in the new country. If you can find such partners, you can answer "yes" to the Capability Gap question.

If you can answer yes to all five questions, you have the key elements of an export strategy.

Part Three. When? has three chapters to help you turn your export strategy into actions that should generate sales:

- **Chapter Eight. Resource the Strategy** offers concepts, cases, and tools to estimate and provide the resources needed to ensure that you can carry out your export strategy. Specifically, these resources include trade finance or other forms of financing needed to set up operations and help provide the cash needed to spur sales in the new country. You also need to determine the skills needed to (1) run the operation in the new country, (2) hire or reassign the appropriate people, and (3) build or rent the systems and other infrastructure required to support them.

- **Chapter Nine. Bridge the Cultural Gap** similarly offers concepts, cases, and tools to help you bridge the inevitable cultural gaps that may emerge between your company and the new country. In general, we have found that it helps to have a manager running the foreign operation to have experience bridging the cultural gap between the home and foreign cultures. And you should assume that the new country will have many fundamental differences, even though we have recommended starting with countries that are culturally similar.
- **Chapter Ten. Take Action** provides a template for you to establish short- and medium-term to-do lists for implementing the export strategy. Such action planning pushes you to form action teams, set priorities, and develop implementation plans that determine key tasks, assign accountable managers and staff, detail specific deliverables for each task, and set deadlines for producing them. The chapter also recommends that you create a process for monitoring the achievement of the action plans, analyze gaps between actual and planned outcomes, and make the appropriate adjustments.

Welcome to the world of exporting. You can profit from it. Read on.

Notes

1. Free trade agreements have been negotiated with Colombia, Peru, Panama, and South Korea.
2. "Poll Results on Trade," *New York Times*, April 2, 2008, http://www.nytimes.com/ref/business/PollResults.html.
3. As a reference, in 2007 U.S. exports to France were US$27.4 billion and U.S. exports to Panama and the DR-CAFTA nations totaled US$26.2 billion. The 2009 and 2010 statistics are from the U.S. Department of Commerce, Office of Trade and Industry Information (OTII), Manufacturing and Services, International Trade Administration, http://tse.export.gov/TSE/TSEHome.aspx.
4. Fourteen FTAs are in effect: with Canada, Mexico, Israel, Jordan, Morocco, Bahrain, Singapore, Chile, Australia, Nicaragua, El Salvador,

Guatemala, Dominican Republic, and Honduras. FTAs with Oman, Peru, and Costa Rica have yet to be implemented. See International Trade Administration, U.S. Department of Commerce, http://tse.export. gov/ for trade statistics.

5. "Table A1. World Merchandise Exports, Production and Gross Domestic Product 1950 to 2009," World Trade Organization, International Trade Statistics, 2010, p. 174, http://www.wto. org/english/res_e/statis_e/its2010_e/its2010_e.pdf; Daniel Ikenson, "Lies, Damned Lies, and Trade Statistics," Cato@Liberty, December 16, 2010, http://www.cato-at-liberty.org/lies-damned-lies-and-trade-statistics/. As Ikenson explains, a recent Asian Development Bank study of global iPhone production illustrates how trade can exceed 100% of GDP. The iPhone leaves China costing some $178, of which only about $6.50 of value was added in China, this being the labor used in assembly. So all of the imports into China as well as the export value are all counted in the trade statistics. Total trade in iPhones and parts is almost double the actual value of iPhones built.

6. Statistics from Economist Intelligence Unit, European Marketing Data and Statistics (London: Euromonitor International, 2007); Economist Intelligence Unit, International Marketing Data and Statistics (London: Euromonitor International, 2007); and Visa International.

7. Manufacturing in the United States can be defined by two seemingly contradictory trends: the output of U.S. manufacturing is the highest it has ever been, putting to rest the idea that America's manufacturing is in decline. However, employment in manufacturing—as a percentage of the work force—has been in decline in the United States for over fifty years, which contributes to the view that the United States is in decline overall.

8. International Monetary Fund, World Economic Outlook Database, 2006, accessed April 2007.

9. Frances Cairncross, *The Death of Distance: How the Communications Revolution Is Changing Our Lives* (Cambridge, MA: Harvard Business School Press, 2001).

10. The WTO reports that "Regional Trade Agreements (RTAs) have become in recent years a very prominent feature of the Multilateral Trading System (MTS). The surge in RTAs has continued unabated since the early 1990s. Some 368 RTAs have been notified to the GATT/WTO up to December 2006. ... At that same date, 215 agreements were in force. If we take into account RTAs which are in force but have not been notified, those signed but not yet in force, those currently being negotiated, and those in the proposal stage, we arrive at a figure of close to 400 RTAs which are scheduled to be implemented by 2010." "Regional Trade Agreements," World

Trade Organization, http://www.wto.org/english/tratop_e region_e/region_e.htm.

11. U.S. Department of Commerce, Office of Trade and Industry Information (OTII), Manufacturing and Services, International Trade Administration, http://tse.export.gov/TSE/TSEHome.aspx.

12. See Gary H. Jefferson, Albert G.Z. Hu, and Jian Su, "The Sources and Sustainability of China's Economic Growth," *Brookings Papers on Economic Activity*, No. 2, 2006.

13. Jason Leow, "China Exports Could Start to Slow," *Wall Street Journal*, August 6, 2007.

Chapter Two

WHERE ARE *YOU* GOING?

How had it gone so wrong? This was the melancholy reflection of Heinrich Schmidt, senior vice president for sales of a nice mid-size German firm, Legacy Corp. (As noted in Chapter One, the case studies with which we open and close chapters are fictitious, but drawn from real-life situations.) The firm is a well-run and well-regarded manufacturer of machine parts, and over one hundred years old. Customers are satisfied. The products are well regarded in the market. But in 2010, management began to focus on a problem.

If you wanted to be polite about it, you could say that sales were not growing as rapidly in recent years as they had in the earlier days of the firm. If you wanted to be impolite, you would say that sales were, well, flat. So about a year ago Legacy decided to explore new markets.

This was a tough decision, because for all of the firm's strengths, it doesn't have much experience in overseas markets. In fact, Legacy had spent most of the preceding few decades just building out domestic sales. There had occasionally been sales outside their home market, but these were somewhat accidental, in that they were not the result of a systematic marketing campaign. In any event, these overseas sales never amounted to much more than 5 percent of the company's total sales. Almost all of them were to customers from the German home market who had themselves established operations in other EU markets. Thus they were not truly overseas sales, and they were always an afterthought.

This passive approach to foreign sales changed in 2010, when Legacy senior management had a detailed discussion with the board, and the board agreed that the company needed to get serious about developing a new market. With a clear goal, but perhaps without a clear strategy, Heinrich was selected. In fact, he was pretty excited about the selection. He had been with the company for eight years and had risen to be one of the top salesmen. Having regularly won awards and bonuses, he was soon promoted to head of sales for major accounts, which allowed him to manage a sales team and join the leadership team of Legacy. The firm's management had a high regard for Heinrich. Heinrich, in turn, knew the company inside out and was proud and happy to help sell its products.

So he ventured to the Ukraine, and what did he find?

At first, it was pretty slow going adjusting to daily life. The traffic, the language difficulties, the strange currency, the confusing directions and telephone systems—it took several months before Heinrich felt he could get around easily. The early meetings were awkward and inefficient, and there were even a few painful mismatches when it became clear the customer had no interest in Legacy products and the entire meeting was the result of a miscommunication.

But as the months wore on, Heinrich's effectiveness improved. He developed sales targets. He continued his calls. He could see that his products might fit the market, even though there were competitive products and substitutes available. He kept at it.

Looking back, Heinrich remembered the discussions, the sales meetings. They were typically quite pleasant. Indeed, compared to the sales calls in Germany, Ukraine business sometimes seemed slow-paced, but also gracious. He was typically met with broad smiles and the offer of a beverage. The business discussion could not even begin until there was a personal discussion of what had brought him here, his family, and where he grew up. It was all quite pleasant—even charming.

He had one rather lengthy set of discussions with a major national distributor. This man was quite successful, having built up his business over the decades, and was proud of his work and relationships around his country. He had been distributing similar products, some local and some from a competitor, for almost twenty years. He maintained the warehouse and national ordering system, and he seemed like an ideal partner. More important, he was intrigued with Legacy products, and he agreed that in terms of pricing and value for money, the product selection seemed superior to what he currently offered. He asked questions about business plans and seemed pleased as Heinrich explained the strategy to build out the business locally and to eventually train local service personnel and have a parts warehouse.

Now, almost one year into the experiment, there were essentially no orders. How strange that the national distributor—always friendly—invariably stated that the time "was not right." There was no particular time element to the product or the market, so it was difficult to understand what he meant by that remark. Worse, a month after hearing that remark, Heinrich was back in town and tried to make a follow-up appointment. He was politely told that the distributor was not available, but that he wanted Heinrich to come to his annual New Year's party. Though several months away, this event had the reputation of being the grandest event in the area.

There are friendly gestures all around, but no orders.

What was the problem?

We'll come back to Legacy and explore more case-specific causes for this failure (and possible solutions) later in the chapter. Now let's consider the overarching problem, which is a key determinant of exporting success or failure: self-awareness.

Self-Awareness as a Key Business Issue

There is a paradox that firms must grapple with as they embark on their international expansion: a company can achieve a high degree of success in its home market without having fully understood why. Many of the finest firms have grown over the years at home by mastering a certain set of activities to sell a certain set of products. The result is they have been able to expand *organically*, building out production, sales, and reputation over the years.

In entering a new market, a firm must decide to expand *strategically*—to tackle problems not step by step, but in larger increments. And the firm can decide how and when to tackle these new markets. These issues can present substantial challenges to the firm. For the most part, even successful mid-size firms do not have strategic planning units that help them think through these questions.

This chapter attempts to address these core questions by looking at the self-diagnosis a company must undertake before diving into global expansion. This self-awareness matters because many companies perform tasks for traditional reasons or reasons that apply only in the home market. We believe that a company seeking to take its business overseas needs to first do some internal soul-searching and tackle some tough questions so that the leadership fully understands the challenges and goals of new markets.

Many companies have a commendable impulse to go abroad. But an impulse is not a sound basis for business decision making. Companies also need a clear understanding of both their business model and their motives. Questions that need to be answered cover three broad areas:

1. **Motives.** Why do you want to go overseas? Is it simply more sales or are there strategic goals? Companies need to understand their goals and motivations as they go aboard; only then can costs and benefits be aligned. In some respects, the decision to go abroad is similar to a decision surrounding a new product launch or a decision involving capital expenditure. You are going to expend capital and other resources, and you need to understand what the likely return will be.

2. **Commercial logic.** Why do you believe your company will succeed in a new market? Does your company offer

better-quality products or more value than competing firms? This question has to be addressed from the perspective of potential customers in the new market. If there is no product advantage, what can you do to change so your company will offer something valuable and different in that target market, compared to the competition? What precisely are the core competencies of your business? What do you do better than anyone else?

3. **Direct and indirect costs.** Do you have the determination, capital, learning orientation, and patience needed to devise and execute an international strategy? In what way is entering a foreign market different from domestic expansion? The decision to go abroad is also a question of capacity and of opportunity costs. Most businesses have finite capacity and cannot easily increase production. This is true with credit and capital, and it is also true for management focus. A U.S. company with US$100 million in domestic revenue might be very happy to develop US$1 million of new business in Mexico, for example. But would it feel as positive about the new revenue if it required monthly trips to Mexico by a VP of sales? Or what if you have a fixed line of credit and new overseas customers require a disproportionate amount of it?

Key Research Findings on These Issues

In the four cases we examine later in this chapter, we will present the nuances that lead to the following key findings on these three issues:

1. **Motives.** The most common reason that companies go global is to maintain or accelerate revenue growth. In this chapter, we look at three examples. The Swedish retailer H&M saw growth opportunities in the United States and believed it could capture that growth by offering customers there something valuable: high fashion at low prices. Tee Yih Jia, the Singapore-based frozen food maker, decided that it could survive only if it could compete with much larger multinational

corporations. And it decided that the only way to do that was to grow by exporting. Cotton gin refurbisher Chihuahua Cattle & Cotton (CCC) went into the Tanzanian beef production business to tap its network of customers, suppliers, and government officials; to take advantage of an idle facility it could put to work; and to improve Tanzanian agricultural practices.

There are many reasons and benefits for going global beyond these case studies:

(i) *To broaden the product slate*. Some companies cannot offer a full product slate in their home market because some of their line has only limited appeal. By expanding into new markets, the company can now sell in its home market products that are primarily sold in other markets. Home Depot developed a line of furnishings for Mexican households when it entered that market and then realized it could enjoy success selling many of these products in the Mexican-American community back in the United States

(ii) *To improve scale*. Some manufacturers cannot optimize the scale of production if they stay in their home market. Developing additional markets makes better use of equipment and allows companies to better plan workloads.

(iii) *To diversify markets*. Different countries grow at different rates; by developing multiple markets, companies can hedge against natural slowdowns and cyclical problems.

(iv) *To learn and experiment*. Markets have different tastes and preferences, different levels of technology, and different systems for finance and distribution. By attaining success in these different circumstances, companies develop adaptability and feedback mechanisms that can strengthen the entire company. We frequently see that successful international expansion is accompanied by a kind of missionary zeal. This zeal often involves an effort to improve the quality of life for the new venture's customers, employees, suppliers, and communities. We see elements of this in CCC's approach to Tanzania. This approach also implies a certain degree of determination, willingness to learn from mistakes, and acceptance of operating losses.

(v) *To deny territory to the competition.* The points just listed do not take place in isolation. Your competitors are going through the same planning exercise as you are. You need to think through your competitor's activities as well. You cannot necessarily compete in every market—yet.

2. **Commercial logic.** Our research suggests that in order to go global, a business needs a specific type of self-knowledge. The business must understand how it appears not to itself but rather to the customers in the global market in which it hopes to compete. The key thing for managers to realize is that they will be making a significant mistake if they conclude that what works in their home country can be easily transplanted into the overseas market. We frequently find that home market success can only be replicated in a new market after careful adjustments have been made. That being the case, what can you do to change your company's strategy so it will offer that target market something valuable and different from the competition? If the company does a thorough job of analyzing the needs of customers in those overseas markets and can fill a need not met by incumbent competitors there, then it has a good chance of gaining market share in the new market.

3. **Direct and indirect costs.** Executives must ask themselves whether they have the right personal qualities required to succeed in overseas markets. For one thing, most global markets do not share the sense of urgency that pervades the United States marketplace. To succeed overseas, executives must be prepared to invest time in building relationships with potential customers, suppliers, employees, distributors, and the various government officials who might encourage the success of the new venture. Moreover, when going global, executives must be prepared to try things that don't work and then adapt accordingly. Finally, executives must be willing to stomach

losses in the early years until the company gains sufficient scale by learning how to compete in the new market.

Self-Knowledge Case Studies

We examine the challenge of self-knowledge by looking at four case studies, three of them in depth:

- **Tee Yih Jia** started in Singapore as a leading maker of *popiah*, the wheat-based "skin" used to make spring rolls. Tee Yih Jia spent years dominating the popiah market at home before going into overseas markets, from which it obtained 90 percent of its revenues by 2006. The key to its success was a deep knowledge of where its strengths lay and how it could exploit those strengths to create competitively superior customer value in those export markets.
- **H&M** is a Swedish clothing retailer that has expanded outside Sweden—generally achieving tremendous growth despite the 2008–09 global economic contraction. H&M's self-knowledge contributed significantly to this global success. Specifically, H&M did things differently from competitors—keeping a close eye on costs, selling hip fashion at low prices, and running a supply chain that lets it design and get new products to market in two weeks—and those differences created a competitively superior experience for customers in its various global markets.
- **Chihuahua Cattle & Cotton,** a U.S. cotton gin production company based in Georgia, opened up an operation in the east African country of Tanzania. Chihuahua's ability to kick off its operation in Tanzania was also based on a heavy dose of self-knowledge. Specifically, it knew that it could offer value to cattle farmers in Tanzania by teaching them how to bring their product to market much faster. It also knew that it had taken the time to build relationships with Tanzanian farmers and government officials, and that it could obtain the permission it needed to acquire an idle beef processing plant located next to a railroad that could distribute its

product throughout the country. This willingness to blend its strengths with the needs of the Tanzanian market illustrates how self-knowledge can lead to success.

- **Failures of Self-Knowledge: Li Ning and eBay.** Li Ning is a Chinese athletic apparel company that had very little sales success when it entered the U.S. market. eBay, the U.S.-based online auction service, initially led the Chinese market for online auctions, but lost out to TaoBao, a more nimble domestic competitor. Li Ning and eBay failed for similar reasons: they assumed that they knew what was best for their respective global markets, but it turned out that what worked in their home countries led to failure in new markets.

Tee Yih Jia

To survive as a small company, growth is vital. And if that small company competes in a tiny market, the only possible place to experience that growth is outside the home country. This means that the company must learn how to export. But how is that company going to export when its competitors in those new markets are multinational corporations with far greater resources?

That is the challenge that faced Tee Yih Jia's executive chairman, Sam Goi, the entrepreneur who built Tee Yih Jia Food Manufacturing into the well-known frozen food business it is today. And Goi realized soon after acquiring the company that he would not get a return on his investment unless he expanded beyond the Singapore market.

Goi explained that such international expansion was essential for the company's growth: "For companies to grow and compete with multinationals, they must go overseas; if not, there is no way to survive." That was the rationale behind the company's drive into international markets.[1]

(Continued)

Tee Yih Jia (*Continued*)

By 2006, Tee Yih Jia exported at least 90 percent of its products, and 80 percent of its sales came from exports. At the heart of the company's success was a carefully developed export strategy. Goi explained, "If your company wants to go overseas, you must first have a strategy. There's no point going overseas if you're too small. Try concentrating on your local market first. Expand into the neighboring countries after your company has grown."

Goi attributes his company's export success to self-knowledge. Specifically, he built the company's export strategy on three Ss—being small, specialized, and strong. Goi said, "I started out small so that I could handle and understand everything myself. And I specialized in popiah skin. I don't do too many things at one time. We're also strong in markets, quality and know-how. That's very important in winning the market."

Among the many problems Tee Yih Jia overcame when it set its sights on export markets was getting financing for Goi's export strategy. In 1985, he wanted to borrow US$8 million to build a factory in eastern Singapore, but local banks turned him down. Goi recounted, "The local banks didn't lend me any money. They couldn't come to a decision even after two to three months. That was quite a tough time for me."

Goi also struggled to get loans while he was building up his Indonesian business. He recalled, "When you start out as a small company, they question your need for so much money. When you need help, not everybody wants to support you. But when you don't need them, everybody comes to you."

This local resistance to his company's growth spurred him to export. Tee Yih Jia started exporting its products in 1980. For example, Goi initially tapped export opportunities in Australia—convincing restaurant owners in Sydney's Chinatown to replace their spring roll pastry with his company's brand.

But it was not until 1988 that Tee Yih Jia decided it should actually manufacture its products overseas. The reason for that decision was straightforward: the benefits of manufacturing the product in the export market—such as lower transportation costs—exceeded the price of entry. To capture that opportunity, the company paid US$20 million to acquire Main On Foods, a Los Angeles food manufacturing and distribution company. 1988 also marked Tee Yih Jia's first expansion into China—a joint venture with the China Pacific group that built and operated a two-story spring roll, samosa, and biscuit factory in Fujian province.

Goi saw the U.S. market as significant but requiring adjustments, due to the strength of the unions there. "The union is very strong. I had a worker who cut his hand—it was a small cut but he sued us for a lot of money. That is America. You must be very careful. Everyone must protect themselves. The people, market, thinking and taste are different. So you must accept the new things."

Goi offers other important lessons for exporters:

• **Use joint ventures, but recognize them as temporary solutions.** Exporters need a local partner. Said Goi:

When you are not there, do you think your employees will put in their full effort to build up your company? Some will but not many. If they are really successful, they may want to set up their own business. . . . You must know how to control the company. If anything happens, you can buy it over or sell [your stake] to your partner. If you know the business when you

(*Continued*)

Tee Yih Jia (*Continued*)

buy it over, you can help the company grow. If you choose to sell it, you will know the right price to sell.

• **You should segment your target market.** In this case, China presented good opportunities in second-tier cities. Although in the early 1990s it was possible to penetrate the market in larger cities in China, in recent years the local competition has the knowledge and capital to block new entrants. However, Goi believes there are still opportunities to tap into second-tier cities like Wuhan and Hangzhou. "Survey the market first. The opportunities are great. But people in China are very intelligent, so why would they need you? There must be synergy in the joint venture. You must also have your own money, market and know-how and you must have capable people stationed there."

• **Don't become complacent.** Goi tries to constantly improve the quality of his products. Although good connections can help win new customers in export markets, success depends on how well the company maintains those initial customer relationships. To do that, Tee Yih Jia produces quality products and prices them with care. Now Goi is considering a diversification into the air and water treatment markets in China and Russia.

H&M

H&M is a US$2 billion Swedish retailer that has expanded globally. Its success, particularly during the 2008–10 economic downturn, is a testimony to its clear strategic positioning in the retail market and the way it performs critical activities to defend that position as it opens up stores in markets around the world.

H&M was founded as a low-priced retailer but extended its strategy to add rapid fashion innovation—a strategy known as "cheap chic." Its Manhattan stores sell items at an average price of US$18. But although H&M's men's line was popular in Europe, it did not do well in the United States so H&M tailored its stores in New York to the unique tastes of young women in the 15 to 30 age range.[2]

Although H&M tailors its stores to the differences across the markets it serves, its global strategy rests on three pillars. H&M's knowledge of how these three pillars create competitively superior value for the customers it serves in those markets is at the core of its popularity and profits.

Here are the three pillars of H&M's strategy:

1. **Frugality.** H&M controls costs that don't add value. It buys raw materials as cheaply as possible, it discourages its people from flying first or business class or taking taxis, and it allows only a very small number of its employees to have company cell phones. To keep costs down, H&M outsources manufacturing to nine hundred garment shops located in twenty-one low-wage countries like Bangladesh, China, and Turkey.

2. **Fashion.** H&M's aversion to costs extends to its attitude toward inventory, which it strives to minimize. This means that it tries to turn over fashions very quickly—introducing products that sell and moving on. To do that, H&M sniffs out the hottest trends ahead of the fashion mavens and turns them into cheap, trend-setting clothes that customers snap up as soon as they appear on H&M's clothing racks. To that end, all of H&M's merchandise is designed by in-house designers in

(*Continued*)

H&M (*Continued*)

Stockholm—finding inspiration from street trends, films, and flea markets. They work with name designers such as Stella McCartney—and have fantastic licensing deals, offering Star Wars and Superman underwear, Simpsons and Rolling Stones socks.

3. **Tight supply chain.** H&M collaborates with suppliers in its local production offices so that its lead times— the time that elapses from design table to store floor—are a mere two weeks, compared with the nine-month lead times of competitors such as Gap. This gives H&M the ability to produce more items—fewer of which are market duds. H&M can minimize such unpopular items by tapping into its database for itemized sales reports by country, store, and type of merchandise. And depending on the level of popularity of these items, stores can be restocked daily or even hourly.

Although H&M has been very successful in its ambitious strategy to expand outside of Sweden, it has made its share of mistakes. For example, H&M enjoyed a very successful store launch on Manhattan's Fifth Avenue, but in 2000 it had problems with stores it opened in malls. For example, that year it opened a 5,400-square-meter store in Syracuse, and its top floor was empty by 2002. It also stumbled in locating an H&M at another mall store in Newark, New Jersey next to other low-priced brands like Express, Old Navy, and Wet Seal, making it hard for H&M to differentiate itself.

But H&M learned important lessons from these mistakes. It decided to shun these 1970s-style malls and locate new stories in more upscale malls and busy downtown locations. In so doing, H&M anticipated cutting its losses in half and ultimately generating a profit from its U.S. stores by the end of 2002.

H&M kept the pressure on itself for growth. In December 2010, H&M's board chairman, Stefan Persson, told the Swedish business daily *Dagens Industri* (DI) that he expected a portion of that growth to come from exporting into countries where H&M did not then have a presence. South America, for one, was an enormous market and a potential new market for H&M.

As Persson considered further expansion late in 2010, H&M was resting on a broad base of global stores. Specifically, it had two thousand stores in thirty-eight countries across Europe, North America, the Middle East, and Asia. Moreover, it had two hundred stores in the U.S. market and opened a new store in Las Vegas in mid-December. In addition to South America, Australia and Africa were also possibilities.

The H&M case offers important lessons on corporate self-knowledge:

1. Know why you're going global. H&M decided to go global for the growth. But in so doing, it did not sacrifice profitability over the long run. However, H&M suffered initial losses from its global strategy. H&M's success sprang from its clear goals—for example, in 2002 it wanted to expand into two new countries a year—and its willingness to learn and adapt to the differences between its home market and the requirements of the new ones it entered.

2. Know how customers and employees perceive you. H&M knew its customers and how they perceived the brand. What is interesting about H&M is that its customers in Stockholm were fundamentally different from those in Manhattan. Nevertheless, certain core elements of H&M's value chain—its emphasis on low costs, its extremely tight lead times, and its ability to get ahead of fashion trends—enabled it to succeed in markets outside

(*Continued*)

H&M (*Continued*)

Sweden. In general, H&M's selection of items in the stores, prices, and quick restocking of stores with popular items created a competitively superior value proposition for U.S. consumers.

3. Accept that missteps will occur and learn from them. H&M initially made some bad decisions about where to locate stores in the United States, and it changed its approach to align its locations with its fifteen- to thirty-year-old female customers. It also learned that American men were not buying the same items that Swedish men did in H&M's stores. So H&M changed the items it sold to better match the desires of its loyal U.S. female customers.

The Contrarian Example: Chihuahua Cattle & Cotton

It's hard enough adapting your *current* business to a foreign market. That's why we generally do not recommend that you go into a foreign market with a different product than what you're used to producing, selling, and servicing. But in rare instances—such as when you have relationships with key players in the foreign country—it may make sense to export a new product to that country.

Chihuahua Cattle & Cotton (CCC) has been operating globally for over twenty-five years. It sells cotton gins in twenty-two countries. In 2007 CCC's CEO, Gary Stowe, decided to begin operating a beef production company in Tanzania. Stowe had two goals: to make a profit and to modernize Tanzania's agricultural sector.[3]

Stowe's core business is buying ten- to fifteen-year-old U.S. cotton gins that are obsolete due to new technology, refurbishing them, and selling them globally through agents in twenty-two countries. Prior to starting CCC, Stowe lived for fifteen years in Chihuahua, Mexico, importing cattle into the United States.

Stowe came up with the idea to produce beef based on the ten years he spent traveling throughout Africa performing sales and service for CCC's cotton gins. In Tanzania, he saw large numbers of cattle on the streets and noted that beef prices were cheap. He learned of a meat-packing plant whose construction had begun in 1978 but petered out when the owner had run out of money and abandoned it 85 percent of the way to completion. Despite the additional investment required to complete construction, the plant was well-located—near a rail line and electrical power cables. Stowe could see the potential.

To get started with the beef production, Stowe founded a joint venture called Triple S Beef in Shinyanga, Tanzania. His goals were to sell local beef in Tanzania, get the facility up to European and American standards, export to the Middle East, and eventually sell to the European and U.S. markets.

Achieving these goals, Stowe realized, would require partners. He spoke with the Tanzanian government to obtain a bid document for the meat-packing plant. He spoke with investors and worked with a company to develop a business plan. His goal was to raise US$30 million to get the facility into operation by the second quarter of 2008. And he anticipated the need to raise US$300 million before the plant would be profitable—which he projected would happen around 2013 or 2015.

(Continued)

The Contrarian Example: Chihuahua Cattle & Cotton
(*Continued*)

When it came to operating a Tanzanian meat packing plant from a Georgia-based company, Tanzania appeared to present a mixture of strengths and weaknesses. Among the strengths Stowe enumerated were familiarity with English, a good cell phone network, a large labor force willing to accept relatively low pay, and inexpensive beef.

But the weaknesses presented Stowe with significant challenges. There was no irrigation in the region, so CCC planned to drill its own wells. The plant lacked refrigeration, so Stowe would provide it in the plant and in its trucks. And the facility lacked machinery and supplies; Stowe would have to import these.

Stowe appeared to have goals for the project that extended beyond business economics. He wanted to help local workers, farmers, and producers and was willing to incur additional costs to achieve that goal. For example, he wanted to give workers health care, education, and training and to make them part of a corporate family. He aspired to offer training in modern farming, ranching, and meatpacking techniques. He hoped to present local cattle farmers with genetic improvement programs and to teach them ways to save energy and water. Finally, he wanted to show local producers how to improve their production and health standards while cutting the time required to bring cattle to market from five years to six months.

Unfortunately for CCC's ambitious plans in Tanzania, Stowe was unable to obtain the financing required to pay for his Tanzanian beef processing plant, so his plans were shelved.

The CCC case offers some critical lessons about self-knowledge:

• **Core competency may cross industries.** CCC has several competencies. One is in its stated business of refurbishing cotton gins. But over time it developed a core competency in African business practices; more specifically, Tanzanian business practices. The company learned how to work with the Tanzanian government, understand risk in Tanzania, and navigate local challenges. The key lesson here is that Stowe's confidence was justified by his knowledge of the local opportunities and challenges. We would not recommend that just any U.S. company trot off to Tanzania to open a beef processing plant, but if a company has mastered specific business skills of operating in a challenging environment, it can improve its odds of success even in a different line of business.

• **Acknowledge your weaknesses quickly and partner to overcome them.** An important part of self-knowledge is assessing the requirements for success on a project and figuring out which of those key skills you lack. Stowe demonstrated this ability when he decided to partner with others to develop a business plan, to raise capital, and to run the operation on a day-to-day basis. In addition, Stowe's relationships with the key stakeholders and his experience starting up new operations in foreign countries gave him an edge in coordinating these partners remotely. We discuss partnerships at greater length in Chapter Seven.

• **Expect to invest in building trust relationships.** As with the Tee Yih Jia and H&M cases, a key lesson from CCC is that going global takes patience. In the Tanzanians, Stowe found distinct differences from people in the United States. They want to take time to build relationships before doing business, and they want detailed information. Although the time required to achieve this level of comfort might be viewed as a delay by U.S. business people, it is really another part of the investment needed to gain access to the business opportunity.

Failure Mini-Cases: Li Ning and eBay to China

Not all companies succeed in their efforts to go global. Two mini-cases indicate that a failure of self-knowledge can be an important factor contributing to such failure. Li Ning is a Chinese apparel maker that failed in its efforts to compete in the U.S. market. And eBay also failed in its quest to gain market share in China when it tried to apply the same strategy it used in the United States. In both cases, a failure to view the company through the eyes of customers in the foreign markets doomed the expansion effort.

Li Ning competes with Adidas and Nike in China, and its eponymous founder was one of the most famous sports figures in China even before he was selected to run around the "Bird's Nest" to light the Olympic flame in 2008. Li Ning's success in China is based on its positioning as a premium Chinese brand rather than the cheapest or the most innovative.[4]

But when it entered the United States, the company thought that it would not need to spend much on marketing because Li Ning's fame in China would transfer easily to the United States. As a result, the company did not invest in a well-known celebrity endorser. Instead, Li Ning chose a relative unknown—Damon Jones, who had played for ten different professional teams in a generally undistinguished NBA career. His name did not resonate with teenage boys as did Nike's endorsers LeBron James, Tiger Woods, or Michael Phelps. Li Ning's failure to view itself from its customers' perspective resulted in low North American sales.

eBay made a similar mistake when it entered China. Things started off well enough; the company acquired a Chinese, online auction service, EachNet. But after acquiring EachNet, eBay managed it from its California headquarters. Thanks to eBay's dominant position in the U.S.

market, eBay executives concluded that they knew better how to attain similar China-market dominance. Just as Li Ning's efforts to apply its China strategy to the United States failed, so did eBay's attempts to force its U.S. strategy on China. The result was that eBay lost its lead in China and Alibaba's Taobao service took eBay's share.

These failure cases reinforce an important message of this chapter: executives considering a global market expansion must know how their company looks to potential customers in the new market. If the company offers a product or service that is more valuable to customers than what competitors provide, then it stands a far better chance of gaining export market share.

Gaining the Self-Knowledge to Take Overseas Market Share

So how can executives gain the self-knowledge they need to determine whether they can profitably take their show on the road? Here's a three-step methodology to consider following:

1. **Decide why you want to go global.** In this step, your company needs to determine the benefits of going global. Our case studies suggest that growth is a good reason. But you ought to set specific growth targets, such as boosting overall revenues from overseas markets to a specific percentage by a particular year. And it makes sense to assess how realistic these targets are by diving into some detailed analysis of the size of the market opportunity and what market share you can expect to gain over time.

2. **Analyze whether you have the specific skills needed to succeed in foreign markets.** The next step in knowing yourself is to make an objective assessment of whether your company has the skills—such as product design, manufacturing, logistics, marketing, and customer service—it needs to succeed in the export market. We devote several later chapters to a more detailed assessment of this question, but you can save yourself a

significant amount of time and money by doing a more general analysis at this stage. To do this, it may help to ask an independent analyst to help you answer two questions: (1) At what skills does your company excel in its home market? (2) How valuable are these skills likely to be in the export market? As Stowe's experience shows, one of the key skills needed to export successfully is the ability to raise the capital to finance the strategy. Stowe's experience suggests he lacked those skills.

3. **Determine whether you have or can get the management talent needed for export success.** If you have a clear reason for wanting to export and your excellent skills in your home market will help you capture export market share, there is one more test of self-knowledge that your company ought to take. The final self-assessment question is whether you have or can get the management talent you'll need for export success. Although the skills that such a manager will need are likely to vary depending on the country, the eBay case is one of many that suggest it is important to not make all the decisions from company headquarters, but instead to delegate them to a manager who knows the foreign market terrain.

Lessons for Legacy Corp.

At the start of this chapter, we introduced you to Legacy Corp. If they had known the lessons we explored here, what might they have done differently? Consider these self-knowledge lessons:

- **Do you really have a good enough relationship with the local distributor to get it to replace its current suppliers?** The local distributor would be concerned about replacing or supplanting his current suppliers. Relationships are important, and he would be loath to "fire" a supplier who had been with him for a while, even if the new importer's products were superior.
- **Can you really offer the post-sales service that customers need in order to use your product?** The new supplier had no repair personnel. How can you fairly sell a product without

repair backup? The local customer would be unhappy with the local distributor, not with the foreign manufacturer.

- **Can you get parts to the local customers fast enough to meet their requirements?** The foreign businessperson may promise to set up a parts warehouse, but this is the same business the distributor is in with his current products. Does the new foreign business envision selling parts directly? If so, why would the local distributor want to carry the product line?

- **Will selling your company's product really enhance your distributor's local prestige?** The local distributor is a successful and proud man. He wants friendships and people he can count on. Simply offering him a "better" product is not enough. The distributor cannot readily replace his current product line without offending longtime business partners. He is unclear whether the new business wants to compete in the parts business, but he is a bit embarrassed to ask. Friendship and hospitality are used to pleasantly mask important business issues. Invitations to large gatherings are a sign of respect, but also a sign the host does not expect to have a serious discussion.

Knowing Yourself Checklist

Do you have all the facts to indicate that your business is an appropriate candidate for an exporting venture? To be able to answer that in the affirmative you ought to be able to answer "Yes" to all six of the following questions.

Questions	Answers (Yes or No)
Do you face growing competition from foreign companies? (If Yes, how can you track this?)	
Are you getting increasing contact and inquiries from potential customers in overseas markets? (If Yes, what data do you keep to measure this?)	

(Continued)

Questions	Answers (Yes or No)
Are you a member of an industry association or a business group that can help arrange a conference or meetings in overseas markets?	
When you describe international expansion opportunities to your corporate leadership, are they enthusiastic?	
If you wanted to dedicate some of your capital expenditure or product development budget to international expansion, could you build a consensus to move ahead?	
Do the majority of your ten largest customers have international operations or expansion plans?	

The U.S. Department of Commerce offers a more detailed checklist that can be helpful for self-assessment.[5] This questionnaire helps you determine whether your company is export-ready by comparing your company's characteristics to those of successful exporters. We believe that this questionnaire offers a useful supplement to the self-assessment tools we present in this and subsequent chapters.

Export Questionnaire

1. Does your company have a product or service that has been successfully sold in the domestic market? ___Yes ___No

2. Does your company have or is your company preparing an international marketing plan with defined goals and strategies? ___Yes ___No

3. Does your company have sufficient production capacity that can be committed to the export market? ___ Yes ___No

4. Does your company have the financial resources to actively support the marketing of your products in the targeted overseas markets? ___Yes ___No

5. Is your company's management committed to developing export markets and willing and able to dedicate staff, time and resources to the process? ___Yes ___No

6. Is your company committed to providing the same level of service given to your domestic customers? ___Yes ___No

7. Does your company have adequate knowledge in modifying product packaging and ingredients to meet foreign import regulations and cultural preferences? ___Yes ___No

8. Does your company have adequate knowledge in shipping its product overseas, such as identifying and selecting international freight forwarders and freight costing? ___Yes ___No

9. Does your company have adequate knowledge of export payment mechanisms, such as developing and negotiating letters of credit? ___Yes ___No

Source: Adapted from Department of Commerce.

Conclusion

The *desire* to go into new markets is almost universal, but the *ability* to go overseas is much more limited. Weak managers confuse the desire with the ability and assume that because they are earnest about the goal they will necessarily succeed. The point of this chapter is to remind you that although you must begin with the desire, successful international execution is a serious business undertaking that demands self-awareness.

Going overseas is a great opportunity—but it is also a potential risk. To determine whether the opportunity exceeds the risk, executives must figure out whether they can offer a uniquely valuable product or service to customers in those overseas markets. This kind of self-knowledge—viewing your company from the perspective of potential customers, employees, partners, and others—will help you to seize the opportunities and minimize the risks of going global.

Notes

1. The Tee Yih Jia case is drawn from Crystal Neo, "From Small Business to Strong Survivor," *Business Times*, July 27, 2006, http://www.asiaone.com/asia1portal/2006/IA/bluesky_IA060802/ Blue%20Sky_files/Blue%20Sky%20-%2003_From%20small%20 business%20to%20strong%20survivor.htm. All quotes are from that source. The authors also sourced information through interviews with Sam Goi.

2. The H&M case draws on Kerry Capell, "Hip H&M," *Businessweek*, November 11, 2002, http://www.businessweek.com/magazine/ content/02_45/b3807010.htm; and "H&M Chair Names South America as Potential New Market," *Trading Markets*, December 9, 2010, http://www.tradingmarkets.com/news/stock-alert/hmrzf_h-amp-m-chair-names-south-america-as-potential-new-market-1357561.html.

3. The Chihuahua Cattle & Cotton case is drawn from Gary Stowe, interview with Peter Cohan, December 17, 2010; and Karen Klein, "Going Global: From Georgia to Tanzania," *Businessweek*, October 10, 2007, http://www.businessweek.com/print/smallbiz/content/oct2007/ sb20071010_810304.htm.

4. The Li Ning and eBay cases are drawn from Shaun Rein, "Lessons for Chinese Companies as They Go Global," *Businessweek*, December 1, 2008, http://www.businessweek.com/globalbiz/content/dec2008/gb2008121 _644935.htm.

5. Department of Commerce, "Export Questionnaire," *Export.gov*, accessed August 13, 2010, http://hq-intranet04.ita.doc.gov/bid/export _questionnaire.asp.

PART TWO

HOW: FIVE KEYS TO CHOOSING YOUR EXPORT STRATEGY

Chapter Three

COUNTRY: PICK THE RIGHT ONE

Marianne was certain. She had done her homework. She had done several months of research. She'd spent a fair amount of time online and going through various specialty publications, all to prepare her presentation to the company's management committee.

The answer was Brazil.

Marianne's company was a small agricultural equipment company in France, Irrigation Corp. Small, but fast-growing—its sales were now over US$50 million a year, and this from a start-up only nine years before. The company designed and manufactured specialty valves used in agricultural irrigation, in which water flow measurement is vital to producing yields. The good news was that the firm enjoyed strong growth within the French agricultural market; the bad news was that it was rapidly approaching full maturity within that market.

Fortunately, the management committee had seen this coming and asked Marianne to lead the effort to design an international study. Although Marianne was a math major, she had shown strong management acumen as director of operations for the company. As the sales force consisted of only three full-time locals plus a few people on commission, it really fell to Marianne to devise the strategy.

For Marianne, the strategy was not too different, perhaps, from one of her math problems. Where was the opportunity?

Brazil represented one of the fastest-growing agricultural sectors in the world, and at the same time it was underinvested. If you looked at the amount of capital in a Brazilian farm, you would conclude that a better irrigation system could well contribute to increased yields. For Marianne, this was 2 + 2 = 4. So it was with no small degree of self-confidence that Marianne presented to the firm's management committee. She even found small Brazilian flags to post on the table.

"Yes, but who do you know in Brazil?" was the first response after her presentation.

Marianne did not fully understand the question and said as much. "It is not a social adventure we are after, it is market opportunity. It doesn't matter who we know; what matters is the demand."

The second question was no less skeptical: "How many times have you visited Brazil?"

Marianne pushed back again: "This is not a holiday, it is business. You can visit Paris forty times and not have one customer. You can go to Brazil and have an order ticket written on the plane ride over."

It seemed everyone in the meeting had a different opinion. The CEO was fluent in English and spent his holidays in London. To him, Britain was the obvious choice. Another person suggested Belgium as closer. The CFO said Russia had a larger agricultural sector than Brazil and was in even greater need of agricultural technology.

The meeting ran over its one hour scheduled time, and finally, at two and a half hours, the chairman adjourned the meeting as the management committee was unable to reach a decision. Although the atmosphere remained reasonably friendly, the committee was split between those who wanted to follow Marianne to Brazil and those who thought the move was too aggressive.

Key Business Issues for Picking the Right Country

In selecting a target country, businesses are faced with two somewhat competing goals: feasibility and value. In other words, how does one assess the likelihood of business success in the target country? And how does one assess the ultimate market size of the target country? In this chapter we primarily discuss the question of feasibility, as we believe a targeting decision initially should be driven by the degree of difficulty. As a firm grows in international experience, it can move to tackle more challenging markets. In the opening international moves, the size of the success is less important than the fact that there has been success.

The subject of value—the ultimate worth of a market—will largely be dealt with in Chapter Five, because that question has much more to do with the domestic market dynamics of the target country.

Let's say you believe Canada will be a promising market for expansion. Ultimately, you will have to commit the capital and the people to test this hypothesis. And after you've committed the resources, either your Canadian operation will lose money and you decide to shut it down, or you'll tread water, or you'll make a profit—in which case you might decide to expand further into Canada or into other countries.

Our point is that the decision to go into new markets should be thought of not as one big, irreversible commitment but as a series of smaller experiments from which you can learn. If the experiments result in commercial success, you can use the lessons from that success to help you explore future opportunities. If the experiment leads to a money-losing operation, you can use the lessons from the failure to consider whether you ought to try expanding elsewhere or can make the operation profitable through informed changes in strategy.

So how do you decide where to expand? You need to answer a series of questions, and the remainder of this book is dedicated to helping you answer them. But the first of these key questions is which country you should target. Our general advice is to stick with a country and a product similar to the ones you know already. So, for example, if you are based in an English-speaking country selling, say, bread, consider branching out to another English-speaking country not too far away and selling your bread there.

We outline how to experiment intelligently, then we explain how we can reduce risk. In general, we view global expansion as a series of—ideally—frugal experiments. Scientific method dictates that you start with a hypothesis—such as *Expanding into Canada will be profitable for our company.* If you can analyze the risks and opportunities of such an expansion before you actually commit resources, you can use the insights gained from the analysis to boost your odds of venturing profitably into Canada.

When businesses expand into new countries, they need to identify up front what's different about getting and keeping customers in that country. But if the company can rely on its previously earned knowledge of customer needs and how to satisfy them better than the competition, then the company can minimize the amount it needs to learn and adapt in order to succeed in a new country.

Continuing with our example, this is not to say that it will be easy or profitable for a U.S. bread company to open up a Canadian branch. To succeed, the U.S. company will still need to determine whether it can work effectively with Canadian distribution channels and offer Canadian consumers a unique product that enough of them are willing to buy.

But by going into the same industry in a related country, you can narrow the zone of uncertainty—that is, the number of business variables that are unfamiliar. And although that smaller zone of uncertainty will not eliminate all the problems of creating a profitable business in the new country, it will make those problems more manageable.

Key Research Findings in Picking the Right Country

Our studies tell us these are the key points to keep in mind when selecting a market:

1. **Don't underestimate the complexities of the new market.** Many countries seem similar, at least superficially. They have similar bus systems, telephones, and hotel lobbies. The currencies seem similar, as do the banks. However, every market

has its own practices; some of these are cultural, others are mandated by law. It is not always easy to discern these differences from the outside. The point is, it's better to start with an easier target than a more complicated one. You are learning. Your company is learning. One problem in many businesses is that everyone wants to run a marathon, but no one wants to run a lap. Start with a country that allows you to run a lap.

2. **Keep it simple.** You don't have to launch your entire product line all at once in the new market. You don't even have to cover the entire new market all at once. Find a distributor who will carry your line. Focus on a handful of stores in a major city. This is a wise way of dipping your toe in the water.

3. **Realize that the end comes from the beginning.** Where you end up is not necessarily where you want to start. We understand the urge for a big start. Ambition is healthy. But even if your goal is to be the top business in China, don't start selling in China if you have not sold overseas before. Start in Hong Kong, or Singapore, both of which are far easier markets for foreigners. You will build expertise with each market. China will still be there when you are ready. Your ability to compete and win in a target market such as China will be improved if you take time to develop international expertise. Entering your target market too early risks setbacks and reputational issues.

4. **Have an incremental business model.** Don't hesitate to start small. We discussed the wisdom of a small product slate earlier. And there are other elements of the business model that can be simplified. You don't need to extend credit in new markets, or extend it in the same way. This may limit your sales, but it might be a wiser way for the first year or two. It will reduce credit risk, and indeed, it could eliminate the need for an entire credit department. You don't need your own warehouse if you can rent one. You don't need your own trucks. You will want to adopt a variable cost structure as widely as possible because it will be difficult to predict how fast business will ramp up. Think about controlling downside risks in a slow market. This might undercut total profits in the early years, but it will also require less cash outlay.

5. **Take advantage of proximity.** If you are an Australian exporter, the United Kingdom is certainly a tempting market. But if you are small, you should probably think of New Zealand first. There are many reasons for this decision, but a key one is that you will be able to hop across the Tasman Sea on short notice, and do so regularly, without it destroying your normal work habits, your sleep hours, and your family life. You simply cannot bounce up to London as regularly. And after you build out New Zealand, you probably want to think about Malaysia and Singapore. In the same vein, pay attention to time zones. An American businessman will be happier to take a 10 A.M. phone call from Mexico than a 10 P.M. phone call from Thailand. Consider our opening example: how easy will it be for Marianne or her colleagues in France to regularly visit Brazil?

6. **Seek homogeneity.** With all of the challenges you will face in your new market, you should avoid venturing into a radically different environment. To the extent you can, reduce language, culture, and currency differences; this will increase your chances of success. There are, of course, many examples of successful businesses in different cultures (think of Toyota in the United States or General Motors in China) but it is just easier to work in a more homogenous environment. Another reason for the Aussie business to start in New Zealand.

7. **Understand trade barriers.** The pattern of trade in the modern era, as we discussed in Chapter One, is one of rapidly declining barriers. However, they still exist in various markets, and you need to understand tariffs and duties as you work through your selection process. Similar, and perhaps more important in this era of low tariffs, are the dreaded non-tariff barriers (NTBs). These are barriers of standards and labeling that can at times be punishing to the exporter. For example, if you manufacture an electrical appliance, what is the standards body in your new market that will certify that your product is safe? If you manufacture a food or a cosmetic product, how will the testing body in the target country evaluate your product?

To keep it simple, you are better off in your early days of international activity in sticking with countries where your country has a Free Trade Agreement or a well-established trading relationship.

8. **Be diligent in your research.** Visit the target country. Talk with businesses there. Talk with banks, law firms, and accounting firms. Visit the commercial section of your embassy. Visit with your national chamber of commerce. Read country reports put out by international banks and think tanks.

9. **Remember the global channels.** Technology now offers mechanisms to market globally even as you pursue a new target market. For example, is your web site enabled to be accessible to foreign customers? This might mean adding options for payment systems and languages. Similarly, can you participate in global trade fairs? Depending on your

---

Global Channels

Depending on your company and your product mix, developing a global channel might also make sense as an export strategy.

By global channel, we mean pursuing an internet strategy to market your goods. Orders can come from any country, which is terrific, but keep in mind this also means complaints and returns can come from any country.

We recommend exploring a global channel if your company currently sells through the Internet, either on its own web site or through other web sites such as eBay, Alibaba, Amazon Shops, or other stores.

If you have enjoyed success with Internet sales, it is worth thinking about how to adjust your web strategy to allow for international sales on the Web. Think about these steps:

1. **Language.** Experiment with making your web site multilingual and allowing the customer to select

(Continued)

the language. A local college can typically provide translation services at a reasonable price. For example, you could hire a native Spanish-speaking teaching assistant to help out with translation and customer email.

2. **Search engines.** Make sure your product and your company can be found in your home market and foreign market search engines. Search for your company and your product in different languages and search engines and see what comes up. You might have to optimize your web content for search engine placement and pay for some internet advertising to improve your reach.

3. **Fields.** Make sure that your web site can handle information from different markets. Phone numbers, postal (zip) codes, and other material can be formatted differently in different markets. Make sure your automated form does not reject for fields that are not filled in or filled in differently.

4. **Servers.** Have your site hosted on a server that is easily accessible to customers in your target country. This will make it quicker for your customers to get product information and make purchases.

5. **China.** ExportNow.com is a U.S. company launching in 2011 by Frank Lavin, coauthor of this book. The company will allow U.S. (and other) firms to easily sell to China on the Internet. ExportNow.com provides English language access and support to Taobao, the largest B2C site in China, with over two hundred million users. By signing up through ExportNow.com, businesses around the world can sell into Taobao using English and conducting transactions in U.S. dollars. It's not a perfect system for everyone, but for many this will be much easier than attempting to conduct business in Chinese and using renminbi (Chinese currency). (For more information, visit www .ExportNow.com.)

industry sector, you might find a range of international customers at these exhibitions.

The Importance of Picking the Right Country: Case Studies

Let's take a look at three examples that illustrate why you must research and carefully select a country for your export venture.

- **Indian drug makers seek American consumers** highlights the importance of looking beneath the surface when considering whether to bet on a new country. Simply put, this case shows how critical it is to know whether you can meet the needs of customers in the foreign country and whether you understand the regulatory requirements that determine whether you can sell your product there.
- **Japanese consumer products companies target India** also illustrates the importance of a country's size and growth in the decision whether to go global. This case shows that Japan's government can influence whether its companies will focus on such growth, yet it also relies on its companies' different methods to determine whether they can do what's needed to gain market share.
- **Apex-Pal enters Vietnam** shows why it's important to analyze the flow of capital into an export market as a barometer of future economic growth. It also demonstrates that such capital flows can lead to rising standards of living and changing lifestyles. Such changes can create fresh demand for a company's products if its home market is more developed than the emerging export market.

Before getting into these cases, it is worth pointing out that there are many ways to compete and win in export markets. These cases illustrate that there are other factors far more important than whether you are from a developing country entering a developed market, a developed market entering a developing country, or a developing market entering an even less-developed market.

Indian Drug Makers Seek American Customers

Indian pharmaceutical companies are much smaller and less sophisticated than their American competitors, so how can they successfully compete in the U.S. market? For all of the advantages enjoyed by the U.S. pharmaceutical companies, the Indian companies have at least one strategic advantage. More important, they know how to exploit that advantage in the segment of the market that will be most favorable.

Simply put, this case is a great example of how to compete in a new country by offering a good product at a lower price. This is not always the right strategy for an SME exporting to a new country. But for companies that expect to offer this kind of competitive advantage, this example is worth considering.

The U.S. pharmaceutical companies are among the largest in the world—selling their products globally—but they suffer from significantly higher costs than elsewhere, and those higher costs lead to prices above what many of their customers are willing or able to pay. Not only that, but the American pharmaceutical companies struggle to come up with new drugs, and although the cost of developing those new drugs keeps going up, the success rate does not.

India has the potential to offer these American customers a long-term solution to some of these problems. How so? India can manufacture drugs at a much lower cost than American companies, thanks to its decades of expertise in the generic drug manufacturing business and its lower labor costs. Moreover, India has extensive experience dealing with the Western drug regulators who play such an important role in determining whether a drug in development makes it to the market.

This is not to say that India has the field to itself. For example, China has a strong position in low-cost manufacturing of consumer products for the U.S. market, but it has lacked the deeper expertise needed to do the same in manufacturing drugs.

In a nutshell, Indian drug producers have wagered that competing with American pharmaceutical companies is a risk that it makes sense to take.

One Indian company that decided to go forward with American exports was Sun Pharmaceutical Industries, which in 2009 sold US$880 million worth of generic cancer and epilepsy medicines in the United States. And those sales were expected to grow by 20 percent in 2010, leading Sun to expand a facility in Halol, India to meet the demand.[1]

Thanks to its manufacturing and research skills, Sun finds ways to cut costs out of the process of manufacturing drugs. Its manufacturing facility, which was being expanded to eight hundred thousand square feet, makes difficult-to-manufacture drugs. Sun's ability to make these products at a lower cost draws demand from the United States. Because lower costs are the primary goal of the pharmacy benefits managers (PBMs) who green-light drug purchases for health plans, Indian manufacturers' ability to make approved drugs that meet FDA standards at a much lower cost than U.S. drug manufacturers have gained them access to U.S. customers.

And thanks to the profits that companies like Sun have earned, they can build research facilities that examine new ways to make drugs at lower costs. For example, Sun employs 650 scientists at a laboratory in Gujarat who use expensive machinery to break drugs into their molecular components and rebuild them into less costly formulations that cause fewer side effects (as proven through the use, in early stages, of ten thousand research animals).

(*Continued*)

Indian Drug Makers Seek American Customers
(*Continued*)

Sun is, of course, not the only Indian company that has bet on the U.S. market. In 2009 India exported US$8.3 billion in drugs and services for the pharmaceutical industry—up 25 percent from the 2007–8 fiscal year. And India's overall drug industry was expected to grow 13 percent in 2010, to US$24 billion.

All this growth in the Indian drug industry has been generated not only by its growing dependence on U.S. customers but also from U.S. manufacturers' perceived need to outsource uncompetitive parts of their value chain. The U.S. pharmaceutical companies could end up doing only molecular drug discovery and marketing of drugs while outsourcing the steps in between.

And one way that U.S. manufacturers are doing that outsourcing is to acquire—entirely or in part—the leaders in the Indian drug industry. For example, in 2010 the generic drug business of Piramal Healthcare, a leading Indian drug maker, was bought by Abbott Laboratories for US$3.7 billion (the R&D arm of Piramal, Piramal Lifesciences Limited, was not part of the deal). And in 2009, GlaxoSmithKline partnered with Indian generic drug maker Dr. Reddy's Laboratories, Pfizer teamed up with India's Claris Lifesciences, and Sanofi-Aventis took over Shanthan Biotechnics.

Piramal chairman Ajay G. Piramal estimates that the company can develop new drugs at 10 percent of the US$1 to US$1.5 billion that a U.S. pharmaceutical company must spend. U.S. companies are eager to capture the benefits of these lower costs. Moreover, as more drugs made in India find their way to the United States, the Food and Drug Administration (FDA), which regulates the U.S. drug industry, has opened offices in India.

In early 2009 the FDA opened an office in Delhi, and in June 2009, an office in Mumbai; together these employed twelve full-time staff, including inspectors and technical specialists. The FDA uses these people to make sure that Indian companies meet U.S. standards even as it is actively approving Indian drugs for the U.S. market. To that end, it has issued nine hundred approvals to facilities in India to import drugs or raw materials for the industry to the United States.

The Indian drug industry's decision to take on business from America offers three important lessons for your business:

1. **Go to a country that understands the value of your product,** so you can boost the odds of breaking even on your investment in exporting there. When Indian drug makers decided to sell into the United States, they anticipated that they might make mistakes; however, they concluded that, given the size of the market, they could likely break even on their investment in additional capacity even if they garnered only a tiny share of the market. Sun generated US$800 million in revenue, which accounted for about 10 percent of India's total pharmaceuticals exports to the United States—and those Indian exports represented a third of the American drug industry's sales. The lesson is clear: make sure you target a country whose market for your product is big enough to allow you to earn a return on your investment after taking a fairly small share of the market. Sun's 3 percent of the U.S. market was enough for it to earn a good return.

2. **Go to a country where your skills can lead to lower costs or higher quality than incumbents now provide.** As we will explore further in Chapter Four, a big market alone is not a good enough reason to go after customers in a foreign

(Continued)

Indian Drug Makers Seek American Customers
(*Continued*)

country. Another important factor is your company's ability to offer something distinctively valuable to customers there. For Indian drug companies, the value it offered U.S. customers was good quality at much lower prices. But it would make sense to go into the United States only if a company could offer this value to customers based on its particular capabilities. The Indian drug companies sustain their lower costs by cutting out unnecessary steps from the drug manufacturing process while minimizing negative side effects. The lesson here is that if you are thinking about going into a new market, make sure you can offer customers value and that you can sustain that value by performing critical activities like manufacturing or R&D in a manner that will let you sustain improvement in that customer value proposition.

3. **Go to a country where you understand the regulatory requirements.** Regulatory issues are not equally important in all industries, but they are extremely significant in the drug industry. The Indian drug industry was able to lower its risks of regulatory rejection by getting to know U.S. regulatory requirements. Thanks to the very large number of Indian manufactured drugs that the FDA granted access to the U.S. market, the agency decided that it needed to open up offices in India. This was a sign that, while the FDA was concerned about quality risks, it recognized that India's drug industry was becoming a major exporter to the United States and thus the agency needed to take proactive steps. The lesson: if you are bringing your products to a new country, invest the time to understand the regulatory requirements that you'll need to satisfy.

Japanese Consumer Products Companies Target India

Japan's leading companies—more so than companies in any equivalent advanced economy—respond to direction from a powerful government ministry: the Ministry of Economy, Trade and Industry (METI). One way METI exercises its influence over Japanese companies is by issuing reports—and one such report emphasized a large, untapped opportunity for Japanese companies: the poor in emerging countries. To their credit, Japanese companies don't simply march in the direction that METI pushes them. Instead, they use METI's urging as a place to begin their own analysis of the opportunities that may present themselves to each company, based on the needs of consumers, and whether the company can supply those consumers with a distinctive product.

Many Japanese consumer products companies—ranging from makers of automobiles to soup—decided to take a look at the market opportunity for selling their products to India's poor. A METI report suggested an enormous opportunity that such companies had yet to tap. Specifically, the METI report suggested that the global market of those who make less than US$3,000 annually totaled four billion people and US$5 trillion in 2009 sales. Although such big numbers attracted the attention of these Japanese companies, those emerging markets would satisfy Japan's need for more rapid growth only if the Japanese companies could sell products to these customers profitably.[2]

Different Japanese consumer products companies are developing new products intended to offer compelling value to poor consumers in India. For example, Toyota and Honda developed smaller, less expensive models

(Continued)

Japanese Consumer Products Companies
Target India (*Continued*)

for Indian consumers. To that end, Yoshinori Noritake, Toyota's chief engineer, took at least thirty trips back and forth between India and Japan between 2007 and 2010 to understand how to build a Toyota for the emerging market driver. The result was the Etios, which debuted in December 2010 with an initial price of US$10,870 for the basic model sedan.[3] The Etios Liva, a hatchback version, was set to follow later in 2011.[4]

Toyota spent a significant amount of time during its visits to India in direct contact with its potential consumers. For example, Noritake visited small Indian homes in rural areas and slums, where he learned that Indians have limited parking space but still want to fit their entire family into the vehicle comfortably. Noritake said, "The amount of space in a city defines how large the car can be. The size of the people defines the interiors."[5]

Not all Japanese companies understand how to capture market share in India through methodical customer research. For example, Canon discovered how it could sell products there only by accident. It received a surge in orders for its US$50 home photo-printers in India but did not know why. After some investigation, Canon discovered that many of the printers were going to rural India, where village entrepreneurs used them to start photo businesses. Their customers were local farmers who paid 50 cents to print the photos they had taken from their cell phones.

Having identified the opportunity to support village photography entrepreneurs, Canon has taken a more systematic approach. The company launched a truck fleet that in effect serves as a mobile showroom for Indian small-town residents to view Canon products. The showrooms provide small-town photographers with workshops on how to operate a wedding photography business. Canon's sales and employee count in India doubled between 2007 and 2010, and Canon expects its sales in India to reach US$1 billion by 2015. Alok Bharadwaj, Canon's senior vice president in India, said, "Even the poorest person has to have photos of the wedding of his daughter."[6]

Even the Japanese noodle industry is changing its products to meet the needs of India's poor. For example, in 2009 Nissin Corp. doubled its Indian noodle-making capacity while reducing the size of its noodle packages to broaden the number of Indian consumers who can afford to pay 10 cents per package for its Top Ramen brand. Nissin also added to its Indian workforce—tripling its staff between 2007 and 2010—while creating a specific flavor for eastern India.

Yuji Tabeta, president of Bangalore-based Indo Nissin Foods Ltd., said, "Our parent company realized the big potential India has. Now that we have the infrastructure in place we can get aggressive about expansion."[7] To achieve this, Tabeta notes that Nissin is developing more regional flavors. Overall sales are projected to increase by 50 percent in 2010.

There are three key lessons to be learned from these cases:

1. **Targeting large markets does not always make them profitable.** Japan's METI identified a large opportunity for its consumer products companies and urged them to explore whether they could meet the needs of poor consumers in emerging markets—the largest of which was India. Japanese companies did not blindly follow METI into India. Instead, leading Japanese companies in the automobile, laser printer, and noodle businesses investigated

(Continued)

Japanese Consumer Products Companies Target India (*Continued*)

further. The lesson from these cases is simple: don't go into a new country just because many people live there who could potentially buy your product. Such a large potential market is a promising prospect that companies *may* want to consider for further investigation.

2. Before investing resources in a new country, spend time learning the needs of its consumers. What should you investigate? The three Japanese companies we highlighted each learned more about the needs of consumers there. Toyota appeared to have done significant amounts of homework, spending time with families in small villages to learn what they might want in a car, whereas Canon stumbled into its customer insights. In these two cases, the key lesson is that before considering an investment in a new country, it is worth taking time to learn what potential customers might look for in a new product. We will take a closer look at how to learn about customers in Chapter Four.

3. While understanding the consumer is critical to developing the right product in a new country, a new entrant must also invest in other capabilities. The Japanese companies we describe all added to different capabilities in order to take advantage of the perceived key success factors for serving their target customers in India. Toyota planned to build and sell a vehicle in India that is designed to meet customers' needs at a price they are willing to pay. Canon assembled a fleet of trucks for visiting rural villages and educating local photographers in how to build a business that uses its printers. And Nissin cut its package size and price while adding new flavors to appeal to a wider cross-section of Indian consumers. The general lesson for your company is that if you find a way to change your

company's domestic strategy that will suit the needs of customers in a foreign country, you should go ahead and adapt your strategy. To that advice, we offer a caveat— such a strategy change should be made only if the higher sales and profits likely to result from the change exceed the costs required to put that change into practice.

Apex-Pal Expands into Vietnam

Apex-Pal is a Singapore-based restaurant and catering chain whose offerings span sushi shops, pizza and pasta parlors, and creperies.[8]

Listed on the Singapore Exchange, for the first half of 2010 Apex-Pal earned net profit of US$1.6 million on revenues of US$34.7 million. By 2010, Apex-Pal had nearly one hundred outlets in nine cities across seven countries including its new venture in Vietnam.[9]

In December 2008, Apex-Pal opened its Sakae Sushi product line at Ho Chi Minh City's posh NowZone Fashion Mall, which attracts youthful, trend-conscious consumers. This expansion was part of an overall corporate effort to make Sakae Sushi a global brand.

In choosing Vietnam, Apex-Pal hoped to capitalize on the flow of foreign direct investment (FDI) into the country, which has attracted other food and beverage industry players. Apex-Pal and its partner, Healthy Food Joint Stock Ltd., saw an opportunity to gain a first-mover advantage at an early stage in the developing market in Vietnam. The consumer base was expanding as well; as more Vietnamese women worked outside the home, there was increasing demand for restaurant dining and take-out fare.

(*Continued*)

Apex-Pal Expands into Vietnam (*Continued*)

Apex-Pal sent a team from its Singapore headquarters, including its director for operations, to develop the new restaurant, working with the chef and service staff to ensure a successful debut.

Apex-Pal's entry into the Vietnamese market offers two useful lessons for SMEs:

1. **Pick a country with growth potential.** Apex-Pal recognized that with the flow of FDI into Vietnam there would be greater economic growth, and given its early recognition of the potential, it could gain a first-mover advantage in Vietnam.

2. **Stay close.** Apex-Pal was already established in most of the markets near its Singapore base; Vietnam and Thailand were the only exceptions.

Lessons for Irrigation Corp.

Now, let's return to the example we presented at the outset. What can Irrigation Corp. learn from these three cases? First, if you aim to go global, you must make sure you bring your management team and board along with you. Second, in so doing, you may need to resist the urge to look at only the opportunities of exporting to a new country and to consider with equal rigor the possible problems. Finally, try to avoid getting too much of your ego invested in exporting to a new country. If instead you take a rigorous and inclusive approach to picking the country, you might conclude that your initial argument for entering that country does not stand up to logic.

If we compare this advice with what transpired at Irrigation Corp., we can diagnose these deviations:

• **Failure to establish internal consensus on goals and parameters.** Marianne had done a lot of work, but she had done it all herself. She needed to make sure her management committee was in full agreement on how a target would be measured and evaluated. Her failure to attain that consensus on process meant she would be unable to obtain a consensus on outcome. Marianne could have helped her cause if she had spent some time on interim briefings.

• **Focusing only on the upside and not on the downside.** Initial targeting has to be done with a primary focus on management of cost and risk, not on ultimate market opportunity. Marianne should have been looking at the easiest market to enter, not the most promising. Brazil represented an extraordinary opportunity for this company, but with just US$50 million in total annual sales, could this company afford—in both time and money—to send one or two people away for a week, several times a year?

• **Allowing personal feelings to dominate the debate.** All of us have favorite countries, based on personal experience, family history, or language studies. This gives us a certain familiarity with a country, but it also might lead us to false impressions and blind us to weak spots. Business decisions should be guided by business logic. The CEO's experience in Britain is irrelevant, unless the CEO is personally going to lead the effort. Again, Marianne could have addressed this point of view if she had met with each member of the management committee to review her parameters and to solicit their advice. Then she could have made a preliminary presentation to the management committee, presenting several different countries and offering an evaluation of each. Thus she would have shaped the debate along her parameters, and she would not be responding to a series of ad hoc decisions.

Country Knowledge Checklist

Have you found a country that you're convinced could offer your company a profitable growth opportunity? To answer that question in the affirmative, you ought to be able to answer "Yes" to all six of the following questions.

Questions	Answers (Yes or No)
Does your firm have strong multilingual or multicultural capabilities? (If not, you should first start in homogeneous markets.)	
Considering the constraints of geography, does your firm have the management pool and the travel budget to evaluate countries around the world? (If not, you will need to start closer to home.)	
Have you identified countries that are the strongest trading partners with your home market?	
Do you have formal criteria for evaluating foreign markets? (If not, you may be operating strictly from personal preferences.)	
Do you understand the regulatory differences, if any, between your home country and the export one?	
Do you have an established research mechanism at your company? (If not, you will need to establish a procedure for studying and evaluating new markets.)	

Conclusion

If you want to go global, the first step is to figure out which country best fits your criteria. As we saw in this chapter, the most common move that companies make is to sell their current product or service in a new country—with modifications to suit the needs of customers in that country. You should pick that country based on criteria such as its cultural similarity to the one where your business started, the number of potential customers for your product, the affordable cost of entering the market, and the similarity of its regulatory structure. If you find such a country, you can proceed to the next step: analyzing in greater depth your company's ability to offer customers there a superior value proposition.

Notes

1. The Sun case is drawn from Heather Timmons, "India Expands Role as Drug Producer," *New York Times*, July 6, 2010, http://www.nytimes.com/2010/07/07/business/global/07indiadrug.html.

2. The examples of Japanese consumer products companies related here, unless otherwise noted, are drawn from Eric Bellman, "Japan's Exporters Eye Every Rupee," *Wall Street Journal*, July 7, 2010, http://online.wsj.com/article/SB1000142405274870429360457534306091163380.html.

3. Anirban Chowdhury, Santanu Choudhury, and Dhanya Ann Thoppil, "Toyota's Etios Makes Global Debut in India," *Wall Street Journal,* December 1, 2010, http://online.wsj.com/article/SB10001424052748704594804575648001858446966.html.

4. "25 Hot New Cars: 2011 Upcoming Car Launches in India," Indian CarsBikes, December 30, 2010, http://www.indiancarsbikes .in/auto/2011-toyota-etios-liva-hatchback/.

5. Bellman.

6. Ibid.

7. Ibid.

8. Sakae case details, unless otherwise noted, are drawn from "Sakae Sushi Leaps into Vietnam with New Management Contract," Apex-Pal web site, December 2008, http://www.thenextview.com/ir/docs/83b9869369dde1814825752e002fcba0-1.pdf.

9. "Sakae Holdings Limited Reports 90% Growth in Profit for 1st Half of 2010," Apex-Pal web site, August 12, 2010, http://www.sakaeholdings.com/Files/Sakae_News_Release_Sakae_Sushi_Reports_Profits_for_1st_Half_2010.pdf.

Chapter Four

CUSTOMERS:
HOW THEY DIFFER

José had an assignment that seemed simple, but actually involved several levels of complexity—as he was beginning to discover. José was VP of sales for Glass Corp., an American glass company that manufactured glass for the auto and construction industries. José's assignment was to help his company develop sales in Mexico.

José was the right person for the job. He had been with the glass company for eleven years, rising from management trainee to the senior ranks. He knew the company, he knew the products, and he was strong at sales. Plus, José was fluent in English and Spanish.

The company was already selling into the auto industry in Mexico because its customers were the same U.S. and Japanese auto manufacturers to whom they sold in the United States. However, the company had no sales in the larger construction industry. José's mission was to build those sales.

Through industry contacts and friends, José spent about a week in Monterrey and Mexico City, meeting with developers and construction companies to get a sense of their use of glass in construction and their purchasing patterns.

He returned to his company with a few key points that he shared in a management memo:

We have several changes we need to implement in our sales approach as we move into Mexico.

- We need to ensure that our building glass is approved by Mexican safety authorities and that it meets Mexico building codes. This is a reasonably simple process, but we are told it will take between one and two months and might involve up to $10,000 in legal fees.
- We need to have a warehouse in Mexico, as local builders will want the supply assurance. They will not want to wait several weeks for special orders from the United States. I will visit with our U.S. inventory supply team to get estimates on the cost of a start-up warehouse.
- We need to be aware that payments in Mexico may be handled differently from what's customary in the United States. Payments for large-scale projects may start only when the building is complete, or they may follow a progress payment plan as in the United States. My advice is that we show flexibility on this point, at least to start with, so that we do not risk losing business by sticking to our current system.

José's memo prompted discussions at headquarters, and senior management took a generally favorable view. The company's success to date in the auto market in Mexico meant they were comfortable with operating in that country, and they understood currency risk, remittances, and so on. They gave José a green light to prepare a budget for Mexico.

José charged ahead, and in only a few months the company was operational in Mexico. José came in under budget.

But where were the sales?

Key Business Issues for Understanding Your Customers in Foreign Markets

Wait a second—*of course* you understand your customers. You have been doing business for thirty years in your market. You know them backward and forward, you socialize with them, you have grown as they have grown, and when they suffer setbacks, so do you.

That is precisely our point: the street truth that you have acquired through years of customer contact does not exist in the new market. You *don't* know those customers—and they don't know you.

And it is worse than just lack of awareness. Customers in different countries can behave differently. Different societies can be visibly different in terms of level of prosperity, language, diet, dress, ethnicity, and race. But there are invisible differences as well. We will talk more about bridging the cultural gap in Chapter Nine, but for now, suffice to say there can be stark differences between different countries' cultures regarding consumer spending habits, attitudes toward youth, respect for privacy, and preference for tradition, to mention a few.

Realize, too, that your customers thrive in an ecosystem—a collection of suppliers and complementary businesses called a "value network." So not only can individual behavior be different, but the value network may also be different. Television advertising may be different. Consumer credit may be different. Even minor differences can have an enormous impact on customer behavior.

What went wrong for Glass Corp. in Mexico? It made the single most common mistake that businesses make when they enter new markets: that is, it did nothing. Too many businesses treat a foreign market as if it were precisely the same as their domestic market. Sure, they may change the label because of requirements, or use a different language, but they do not evaluate the new market and new customers and make adjustments accordingly.

If you follow the advice of the previous chapter and are aiming for a market similar to your current one, and one that's nearby, perhaps your adjustments can be minimal. But adjustments must be made. This chapter will help you think through how to approach new customers and new markets and how you can make the necessary alterations in your business to win in the new market.

As we all know, Shanghai ain't Indianapolis. Heck, Toronto ain't Indianapolis.

This chapter explains the critical importance of knowing your customers before investing in global markets. Why is this important? Our discussions with commercial officers at the U.S. Commerce Department reveal that many companies take too casual an attitude toward knowing their customers. They attend a trade fair with potential customers from the country in question, meet a few companies who express interest in buying their product, and decide to sign up with them. Although some companies follow up after their trade fair meeting, many more don't, and they find that not much happens after that. Remember, it often helps to think of those customers as both the end users of your product and the distributors who will sell to the end users.

The nub of the problem is distance and familiarity. In the home market, customers have developed a high degree of familiarity with the company and the product, perhaps extending over decades. The company has grown, evolved, and weathered storms, and there is a degree of comfort that creates a reservoir of good will.

In the new market, however, none of these strengths exist. A new-to-market company must make an extra effort to cultivate goodwill and navigate through problems. The extra burden to develop these relationships will be disproportionately high. A company that wishes to enter a new market must devote extra time and resources, proportionate to sales, to ensure that customers are satisfied.

In a new market, a company does not yet have a brand or a reputation. We tend to underestimate the importance of these vital elements of business success. So in our home market we have a "presumption of innocence," so to speak, because our customers know us and trust us.

In a new market, however, we can face a corresponding "presumption of guilt" because we are an unknown. We have to find the right way of connecting with customers to build that brand loyalty. A company must be prepared to "bulk up" its presence in these new markets with extra visits, extra presence, and extra contacts to build confidence. Indeed, as a new entrant to a market, you should expect to spend a disproportionate amount of time just finding the new customers. Extra marketing and advertising might be required, and additional promotional efforts and extra work with your sales and distributors.

This chapter also explores the fundamental question of how to find a customer. How do you identify your customers in your target market? In your home market, the process of customer identification has evolved over the life of the company. In your target market, you want to move as quickly as possible to identify and contact possible customers. This chapter describes examples of why customer knowledge and familiarity matter, including the following:

- In what ways might your customer base be different from your home market customer base?
- How can you find out what the customers you target need from you before starting to sell to them?
- How can you tell whether your proposed product or service will offer those customers a superior value proposition?
- How should you adapt your domestic business strategy to deliver competitively superior customer value in a foreign market?

Key Research Findings on These Issues

The cases that follow provide different perspectives on these key issues. We summarize them here as follows:

1. **In what ways might your customer base be different from your home market customer base?** To boost your odds of success, pick potential customers in foreign markets who are as similar as possible to the ones in your home market. This will allow you to use an approach for the potential foreign customers that's similar to the one you use for your current domestic ones. However, there are likely to be differences in customer behavior, which then leads to differences in how you market, sell, and service them. Our key recommendation

is that you get to know the potential foreign customers well enough to diagnose and understand these differences.

2. **How can you find out what the customers you target need from you before starting to sell to them?** This depends on the kind of product you're selling. If your product is something that will easily become popular among a large number of end users in the export market, then you simply need to find a distributor that will do a good job of reaching those end users. But if your product is seen as new to that export market, you may need to spend time with that country's so-called early adopters—people who like to be the first ones on the block to own cutting-edge products—to get them excited about the product before you even consider finding distributors. To that end, we examine Tokyopop, a U.S. distributor of Japanese cultural products that figured out a fairly elaborate process for taking what its founder thought would be the most popular content to export from Japan to America and then translating it in a way that would be most appealing to U.S. consumers. We also look at the Chinese clothing retailer eno, which found that the most efficient way to figure out what Chinese teenagers wanted was to hire Chinese designers who intrinsically understood what eno's customers would want, better than its American cofounders ever could.

3. **How can you tell whether your proposed product or service will offer those customers a superior value proposition?** To answer this, it's important to point out that there are two ways to give customers a superior value proposition: (1) by providing a good product at a lower-than-industry-average price or (2) by offering a better product at a higher price. To know whether either of these paths to a superior value proposition make sense for your company, you must understand how you compare to the competition when viewed from the customer's perspective. We look at the furniture rental firm Home Essentials, which got started through a friendly conversation about the limitations of the existing market. The company was able to solve those problems and offer customers better selection and pricing.

4. **How should you adapt your domestic business strategy to deliver competitively superior customer value in a foreign market?** Achieving this goal depends on how well you know your customers' needs and your competition's capabilities. For example, medical products company ResMed adapts its product to the specific needs of its export markets by conducting joint R&D intended to target the different requirements of medical professionals in each market.

Understanding Your Customer: Four Case Studies

This chapter presents the following examples of why such customer knowledge matters:

1. **ResMed,** an Australian medical technology company, was a pioneer in the design and production of breathing systems to help people with various respiratory conditions, primarily sleep apnea. In selling medical devices, ResMed understood that customer behavior was dictated by comfort and trust. The company became a market leader by producing quality equipment, selling a wide range of face mask models and building brand loyalty through targeted marketing campaigns.

2. **eno,** a Chinese youth clothing retailer started by a pair of Americans, has turned itself into a multimillion-dollar business by betting on its designers' superior insights into what China's consumerist teenagers want to buy. eno's American cofounders watched its sales boom when they let go of what they thought they knew about Chinese consumer wants and let their Chinese designers pitch their best ideas.

3. **Tokyopop,** a Los Angeles-based seller of manga (stylized Japanese comic books) to American and other western youth, achieved phenomenal success ($40 million in 2004 sales) since its 1996 startup. Its CEO, Stuart Levy, saw an opening for manga in the United States and researched storylines that would most appeal to American audiences. Levy's knowledge of the U.S. consumer demand for manga has helped him persuade publishers to print and distribute his product. More recently,

he has used that knowledge to partner with companies that produce action figures and cartoons based on his manga content.

4. **Home Essentials,** a U.S.-based furniture rental company that has expanded to serve expatriates in the Middle East and Asia, has succeeded largely due to its understanding of its customers' needs. Moreover, Home Essentials has learned that although many natives in the countries where it operates, such as Dubai and Malaysia, do not naturally favor the idea of renting furniture, the Americans working there for companies like IBM and ExxonMobil think it's a great idea. Nevertheless, because Home Essentials hires people in these countries, it must be sensitive to cultural differences—such as an "employee of the month" award that prompted the embarrassed winner to share his prize with his coworkers.

ResMed

ResMed designs and manufactures facial masks, humidifiers, and flow generators—high-technology air pumps and respiratory ventilators.[1]

With over thirty competing companies in the field of sleep technology, how did ResMed win industry leadership? ResMed ascribes its success at turning a niche medical product into a global leader to two key factors: technology leadership and medical education. In other words, know your partners and your customers.

When it comes to leadership, ResMed is the largest global innovator in the field of breathing technology, with R&D expenses at 7 percent of revenue. Evolution of the technology of masks, flow generators, and humidifiers continues, including a family of computer-controlled products and wireless diagnostics.

ResMed understands that customers with medical problems have a strong preference for high-quality products and that the comfort and fit of these products drive the compliance necessary for clinical benefit. Low-quality products will not gain customer confidence. A range of thirty different designs, each available in multiple sizes, has evolved to conform to individual face shapes and sizes and therapeutic need. The latest is a change to a recent successful design, making it the first mask to target women.

As to the second factor, ResMed realized that its essential partner in education was the medical profession. When the company began exporting in 1989, the ResMed technique was new and not widely recognized by the medical community. The condition being treated was not taken seriously by anyone apart from a few research scientists. There was effectively no market.

If the doctors do not understand your product, the patients won't either. ResMed devoted the bulk of its communication efforts to educate medical professionals who needed to recommend or endorse their products. ResMed used the inventor, a well-known academic, as a publicist, and his name served as a trademark for the product.

ResMed sponsored conferences both in the export market and in the United States, with the inventor a prominent contributor. To keep the company name in front of the profession and to show that the company was abreast of research developments, clinical research literature was collected and distributed to medical leadership. Company staff was kept abreast of medical developments worldwide so they could incorporate best practices into products. The company financed clinical research studies, devised marketing strategies to promote the company as a technology leader, and established a Medical Advisory Board composed of leading international research clinicians.

Twenty years on, these educational and technology activities underpin ResMed's continued success. Medical

(Continued)

ResMed (*Continued*)

literature of some 150 articles per month is still distributed. ResMed sponsors clinical research and conferences, and product development continues unabated. ResMed has over three thousand granted or pending patents and design registrations.

The key lesson of the ResMed case is that winning in foreign markets depends on satisfying two levels of customers. The company cultivates medical professionals through thought leadership, journal articles, patents, and the like. And they meet the needs of end users by offering a range of sizes and styles.

eno

Two Americans formed a partnership in 2006 and went on to find a successful retail clothing company in China that they called eno. In accomplishing this feat, they had to throw out preconceived ideas about how to do business in China. At the core of their success was a willingness to empower Chinese designers to come up with ideas for new products that appealed to Chinese youth.

In this sense, their retail store embodies the core message of this chapter—that to succeed in foreign markets, business leaders must give those customers a product that meets their needs better than the competitors'. And a big part of doing that is realizing where a company's strengths for competing in that foreign market begin and end. Where the strengths end, business leaders must develop the skill of partnering with others who do have the strengths needed to win in that market.

eno's cofounders were U.S. entrepreneurs who decided to offer young Chinese consumers a different retailing experience. Renee Hartmann and Tor Petersen started one of the first brand-name retailers to sell "hip, urban streetwear designed by and for young Chinese." This positioning was unique in China, whose retail clothing market had been dominated by well-known U.S. and European brands and local companies that knocked them off. Hartmann said, "We wanted to create a brand focused 100 percent on China."[2]

Today's Chinese youth know only a China of affluence, a China of 220 million fifteen- to twenty-four-year-olds whose inflation-adjusted per capita disposable income, grew at an average annual rate of 7.2 percent between 1978 and 2009, when it reached US$2,300.

The eno cofounders brought an unusual background to the task of cashing in on this business opportunity to offer Chinese youth a unique retail experience. Neither Hartmann nor Petersen had previous fashion design experience. Petersen was a fluent Mandarin speaker who had spent eight years as a manufacturing and marketing executive for Nike China. And Hartmann had been an investor relations consultant who worked with companies going public in the United States and Hong Kong. Petersen hired Hartmann as CFO in 2005.

By the fall of 2009, their company had achieved considerable success. Three years after it debuted, eno had sixty employees (five of whom were designers), six stores, and three franchises, and its fashions were carried in twenty Chinese department stores. In 2008 eno's sales exceeded US$1 million, and it expected to hit US$2 million in 2009 sales while making a small profit.

eno's path to profitability was not smooth. It was initially founded by three Nike China vets as Zou Marketing, a

(Continued)

eno (*Continued*)

sports brand and event marketing firm. But competition from Nike and Adidas blocked the venture from gaining market traction. eno emerged from a successful pitch to Shanghai venture capital firm Chengwei Ventures that gave the company US$5 million to build China's version of Urban Outfitters.

Hartmann and Petersen launched their new vision for eno by selling T-shirts through partnerships. Specifically, eno partnered with three different fashion industry ecosystem participants: "local artists and musicians, online competitions in which users would submit designs and vote their favorite T-shirt graphics into production, and an internal design team."

But Petersen made a mistake initially: he thought he ought to direct the work of eno's internal designers. Petersen came up with design ideas—such as "preppy" or "Mardi Gras"—but eno's designers did not understand them, and Chinese customers didn't buy the result.

To his credit, Petersen realized that his approach was failing, mostly because he was not tapping into his designers' passion. So he changed eno's design process, making designers responsible for coming up with concepts and pitching them to him. He took a more detached creative role, acknowledging his limited insight into customer needs. Petersen admitted wryly, "After all, we're not Chinese kids."

By letting its Chinese designers get creative and by speeding up the time from design to market, eno prospered. For example, its eno Classic, a series of T-shirts and hooded sweatshirts adorned with variations on an abstract logo created by designer Feng Feng, sold much better than a collection designed under the old system. But the big breakout was a series of "environmentally themed" shirts featuring the Chinese character for forest.

eno borrowed a concept from H&M—developing a supply chain that will allow it to get small batches of new designs out quickly. eno already uses recent sales data to reorder popular styles each week. As Petersen said, "You allow the consumer to tell you which products are working." eno can take a new T-shirt from concept to retail store in three weeks by partnering with small factories located a few hours from Shanghai.

eno's insights into the Chinese consumer are so valuable that other companies are paying for them. To capitalize on that demand, eno created a consulting business called Enovate. Launched with a staff of five in 2009, it consults for companies including Ticketmaster and New Balance, researching the youth market and helping with product design and development.

The eno case reveals some important lessons regarding the importance of understanding consumers in a foreign market and of forging effective partnerships to serve those consumer needs.

1. **Approach a new market's customers with intellectual humility.** A big part of eno's success was willingness to learn from mistakes. The partners quickly recognized that their initial business strategy would not work, and they were flexible enough to try a different strategy: getting to know the needs of Chinese consumers.

2. **Figure out the skills you need to meet foreign customer needs.** eno's cofounders quickly recognized that retailing to young Chinese would work only if they were able to hire local designers and manufacturers who could produce new designs and get them to the stores quickly. eno did a good job of finding the right partners.

3. **Create a climate in which partners can thrive.** eno made a major shift in its design process with the

(Continued)

---

eno (*Continued*)

realization that its U.S.-born CEO's direction of the design process produced product bloopers. Rather than stick to forcing Chinese designers to accept his vision of designs, Petersen let his Chinese designers create what they thought eno's customers would buy. Because the Chinese designers knew the customers better than Petersen, their designs clicked—and the company grew.

4. **Expand from your strengths.** Although eno is far from an expert on Chinese consumer needs, it knows more than many other U.S. companies. eno has been successful in turning that superior knowledge into a new source of revenue. Because U.S. companies value that knowledge of Chinese consumers, they are willing to pay eno to help them build out their businesses in China.

5. **Don't let initial failure get in your way.** The eno team kept pressing on even after a series of setbacks.

Tokyopop

An American business executive goes to Tokyo in 1991, falls in love with a uniquely Japanese product, and five years later convinces Americans to buy into his love of that product—to the tune of US$100 million a year and 50-percent annual growth. At the core of this success is the executive's ability to identify which attributes of that product will appeal to particular American customers.

That company is Tokyopop. Due in no small part to Tokyopop's success, in 2003 Americans bought US$40 million worth of manga—Japanese illustrated novels depicting "violent, boy-friendly superhero tales; love stories for teen girls"[3]; and business dramas for adults. Tokyopop's founder and CEO is Stuart Levy, a lawyer with no publishing experience who "transformed manga into a $100 million U.S. industry."[4] Levy founded the company in 1996 and built it into America's leading seller of manga—overseeing a doubling of sales each year and as of 2004, reaching five hundred titles in print, with projections of 50-percent annual growth.

Levy created the U.S. market for manga by tapping U.S. consumers' excitement over anime TV shows based on animated Japanese-style cartoons. When Levy went to Tokyo to eat sushi, he fell in love with manga's visual appeal and broad subject range. Levy also noticed that manga appealed to both men and women of a wide range of ages. So he convinced Barnes & Noble to carry standardized manga books—5-by-7.5-inch, US$10 paperbacks.

Tokyopop's process for figuring out which Japanese manga will work in the U.S. market offers an excellent example of how to successfully adapt a product from one culture to customers in a different one. Tokyopop has a green-light committee in Japan that evaluates manga titles it thinks will appeal to American consumers. Those nominated titles then go to Tokyopop's Los Angeles office, where non-Japanese-speaking employees consider the graphics and a text synopsis to assess their likely popularity.

Tokyopop also has a rigorous process for measuring the popularity of its titles. It emails a hundred thousand customers each month to measure reader interest, and it monitors newsgroups and chat rooms to identify trends. Tokyopop then "brings in a freelance translator and an in-house rewriter to add U.S. slang and colloquialisms."[5] During production, all details of the books reside in a database that allows employees in Tokyo and

(*Continued*)

Tokyopop (*Continued*)

the United States to track the book production process as it evolves.

Using this system, Tokyopop planned further global expansion. It sought to sell its products in Germany and Britain in 2004 and to market original editions in Japan in 2005. (Although it did enter the Japanese market, in mid-2008 Tokyopop was forced to restructure its Japan division due to slowing sales during the financial crisis, intense competition, and a shift in its service to videos and mobile distribution.[6])

The company also expanded its content into new forms—signing a deal with Hasbro to produce action figures for Tokyopop's *Rave Master* animated show, which debuted on the Cartoon Network in 2004. And it negotiated a license for exclusive rights to publish any manga books based on Disney's movies and TV shows.

But the Tokyopop story took a turn for the worse in 2011. Among its biggest problems was the bankruptcy of a major retailer, Borders. Moreover, in February 2011, Tokyopop chief operating officer and publisher John Parker resigned from the company.[7] With his departure, only three of the original founders remained: Stu Levy, CEO; Mike Kiley, HR manager and publisher; and Victor Chin, VP of inventory. More layoffs were anticipated by March 2011 as Borders stopped paying publishers, and it was expected that Tokyopop would end 2011 with around twelve employees—a fraction of its 2007 peak of one hundred.[8]

The most important lesson from the Tokyopop story is that it takes imagination and discipline to port a product across cultures and make money doing it. Levy believed that there would be many other Americans who would be willing to buy manga books, and he was able to persuade a big U.S. retailer of that potential. He then created a rigorous process for picking the specific Japanese content that would most appeal to those American customers. And he set up systems so that employees in Japan and the United States could track the progress of creating each book and assess what customers liked and how their interests were evolving. However, the unhappy ending of this story suggests that a company must continue adapting effectively to changing industry requirements. Tokyopop has not done so.

Home Essentials

Americans working for their companies in faraway places like Dubai and Malaysia don't want to own the furniture in their temporary living quarters. An American firm based in Dallas decided that it could solve the problem facing these customers by renting them furniture; when the expatriates left to work elsewhere, they could conveniently return their rented furniture instead of having to lug it to their next posting.

Chris Exline, a Dallas, Texas–based owner of a furniture rental store, realized there was an opportunity to export his concept when he heard a friend's story. The friend's employer had given him US$5,000 to buy appliances that would work with Singapore's electrical system. But the friend then had to declare that money as taxable income. Exline pointed out that if he rented furniture instead, he could get a tax deduction. Exline wrote a business plan for a new venture called Home Essentials, which Exline founded in 1998. By 2005 it was operating in

(*Continued*)

Home Essentials (*Continued*)

Dubai, Hong Kong, Kuala Lumpur, Malaysia, Singapore, and Baghdad.[9]

Furniture rental is a big business in the United States—with US$6 billion in 2004 sales—but it does not exist in most other countries. As a result, Exline does not face direct competition in places like Hong Kong. When Home Essentials opened its second foreign office in 1998, Chinese journalists interviewed people on the street with video cameras to capture the stunned look on their faces when they were asked, "Would you ever rent furniture?"

But Home Essentials focuses on a different segment of customers in the countries where it operates—not the person on the street, but multinational companies like Ernst & Young and IBM, and the local landlords who rent apartments to them. It's much less expensive for these Home Essentials customers to rent furnishings for several hundred dollars a month than to spend tens of thousands of dollars to ship workers' furniture in containers—which takes six to eight weeks.

To expand into new markets, Home Essentials follows its customers. In March 2003 Exline was flying from Tokyo to Hong Kong when he read that the United States intended to spend billions of dollars on the rebuilding effort in Iraq. Seeing a potentially huge need for imported furniture, Exline opened an office in Dubai six months later and in March 2004 began operations in Baghdad.

With persistence, Exline was able to win an initial US$90,000 contract for beds, dressers, nightstands, and sofas for the U.S. Agency for International Development employees' homes. But getting that order was hardly a slam dunk. He first met people in Dubai who knew people in Iraq, and then found a way to reach Baghdad from Jordan. Exline paid several visits to the headquarters of the American Coalition Provisional Authority and eventually won their trust.

Home Essentials has achieved considerable financial success. Launching with Exline's initial investment—$750,000 of his own money—Home Essentials became profitable in 2001 and reached US$3.5 million in sales by 2003, doubling to US$7 million in 2004.

The Home Essentials case offers a good conclusion to the cases in this chapter, because it highlights the importance of a simple idea: know the needs of your customers and offer them a product or service that satisfies those needs better than the competition. Home Essentials has pioneered the international furniture rental approach so effectively that so far no other companies have followed its lead overseas. As long as that's the case and multinationals continue to ship people overseas, Home Essentials can expect to grow along with that flow of expats.

Gaining the Customer Knowledge to Take Overseas Market Share

There is a good chance that your product will be new to customers in the export market. And even if it is not completely new, it is likely that you will need to break through existing networks of customer comfort in order to penetrate the export market. To accomplish such a breakthrough, you will need to gain knowledge that you currently lack.

So what should executives do to acquire the knowledge about potential customers that they need in order to determine whether they can profitably take their show on the road? The experience of Tokyopop and Home Essentials suggest a five-step methodology to consider:

1. **Identify the early adopters in the export market.** If you sell a consumer product like food or clothing, the early adopters

may be students at the largest or most prestigious universities in the country. Talk with commercial officers from your country, embassy staffers, and your university alumni clubs in the export market, among others, to get ideas for finding these early adopters and gaining introductions to them. You may ultimately end up partnering with a distributor, but unless you have talked to these early adopters, chances are you will lack the ammunition you need to convince distributors to carry your product.

2. **Develop a customer interview guide.** Once you've identified the early adopters, the next step is to talk with them. You'll want to prepare carefully for these conversations, organizing your thoughts and questions. To that end, your company should develop a customer interview guide, including questions such as whether the customer buys similar products now, what specific criteria they use to choose among competing suppliers, how they rank these criteria in their importance to the purchase decision, how well they see competitors satisfying those criteria, and whether the customers have any unmet needs.

3. **Create a focus group of potential customers and talk with individual customers.** If you are selling directly to retailers and to consumers, then your task is more complex; within a retailer there may be several individuals who get involved in the decision to distribute a new product. If you're talking with individual end users, the interview guide can help you structure your conversations with them and keep track of what they say.

4. **Once you've completed the interviews, analyze the results of your customer research.** Your analysis may include totaling the various answers and trying to detect patterns. Ideally, your research efforts should help you to figure out specifically how customers choose among suppliers, where your potential competitors are doing a good job, and where they are not doing so well. This analysis should help you to identify an unmet need that your company can satisfy better than any other competitor.

5. **Decide how to position your company to deliver competitively superior value to your target customers.** If you find an unmet need that your can satisfy better than the competition, draw a map that depicts the key criteria that customers use to choose among competing suppliers. Then place your competitors on the various sectors of that map where you think they are strongest. Ideally you should be able to imagine where your company could compete on that map in a space not currently occupied by any competitors.

Lessons for Glass Corp.

Let's return to our opening example of Glass Corp. José did a strong job of identifying differences in business practices between Mexico and the United States for his industry, and he uncovered regulatory, supply chain, and financial challenges. He also estimated the expense required to surmount those obstacles. We rate José's memo as a good first step in market analysis and the type of exercises a business should undertake in evaluating new markets.

However, José visited with only one level of customers—the builders and developers. He did not meet with the ultimate customer—the owners and operators of the buildings. Nor did he meet with the architects and interior design teams that help make decisions on windows. He learned a lot from those with whom he did meet, but he missed a lot by not meeting with a broader group.

Here's one example: given the latitude of Mexico and the strong sun, there is an overwhelming preference for tinted windows for solar control, even in situations in which an equivalent U.S. building would not have tinted glass. Another example: residential glass in Mexico is more likely to contain decorative elements than the purely functional glass found in most U.S. households.

The bad news for José is that he did not pick this up in his analysis of the market. The good news is that as he hired his local sales team, he learned very quickly that the Mexican market would require customized products.

Customer Knowledge Checklist

Did you find an unmet customer need in that foreign market that your company can satisfy better than the competition? To answer that question in the affirmative, you should be able to answer "Yes" to all six of the following questions.

Questions	Answers (Yes or No)
Are customers in the new market similar to customers in your home market?	
Have you identified ways to determine the degree of differences in how the new customers would purchase and use your products, and to evaluate how significant these differences might be?	
Can you use the same sales and distribution channels in the new market as in the home market?	
Do you have an established method for uncovering any differences in customer preferences in the new market and acquiring customer feedback?	
Do you already know how much it costs you to acquire a customer in your home market ?	
Have you identified the additional expenses you must budget for the customer discovery process?	

Conclusion

As you contemplate entering a foreign market, you must realize that you can gain market share only if you're introducing a product that offers uniquely compelling value for potential customers there. It's a mistake to assume that what works for you in your home market will help you compete just as well in an export market. It's better to assume that you know nothing about customers in the export market and that you need to build your knowledge base from scratch. Only by talking to potential customers in the export market can you know for sure what they need—and how well your potential competitors are meeting these customer needs. Through these conversations, you can try to find a shared unmet customer need that you can satisfy better than anyone else in that market. And if you find one, your company needs to assess whether it can compete in that foreign market on its own or whether it needs partners.

In the next chapter, we'll take a detailed look at dealing successfully with your competitors in the export market.

Notes

1. Rob Douglas, COO of ResMed, interviews with Frank Lavin on April 21, 2009, and February 23, 2010, and correspondence.
2. The eno account and all quotes are drawn from Malika Zouhali-Worrall, "China's $treet fashion," *Fortune*, October 29, 2009, http://money.cnn.com/2009/10/29/smallbusiness/china_street_fashion.fsb/index.htm.
3. Julia Boorstin, "License for Adventure TOKYOPOP, Los Angeles," in "Small & Global: Whether They Export Roller Coasters or Import Japanese Novels, Small U.S. Companies Are Conquering the World—Country by Country," *Fortune* Small Business, June 1, 2004, http://money.cnn.com/magazines/fsb/fsb_archive/2004/06/01/373316/index.htm.
4. Ibid.
5. Ibid.
6. "Tokyopop Splits into Two Companies; Cuts Production 50 percent," *ICv2*, June 30, 2008, http://www.icv2.com/articles/news/ 12677.html.
7. "Tokyopop Goes to Diamond for Distribution," The Beat, January 13, 2011, http://www.comicsbeat.com/2011/01/13/tokyopop-goes-to-diamond-for-distribution/.
8. "Tokyopop," Wikipedia, February 12, 2011, http://en.wikipedia.org/wiki/Tokyopop.

9. The Home Essentials case is drawn from Chris Exline's discussions with Frank Lavin and from Julie Sloane, "Following the Action HOME ESSENTIALS, Los Angeles," in "Small & Global: Whether They Export Roller Coasters or Import Japanese Novels, Small U.S. Companies Are Conquering the World—Country by Country," *Fortune* Small Business, June 1, 2004, http://money.cnn.com/magazines/fsb/fsb_arc hive/2004/06/01/373316/index.htm.

Chapter Five

COMPETITORS:
A DIFFERENT MARKET

"It cannot be that hard to sell in Korea, can it? They have bathrooms there, right? They use them just like we use them, right?" The CEO was peppering his leadership with questions as the company was trying to tackle the Korean market. The firm, Fixture Corp., was a smallish Canadian firm that in twenty years had grown from a household plumbing business to a niche manufacturer of specialty valves and equipment used in bathroom fixtures. It was now one of the largest manufacturers in this sector in Canada, though sales were only around US$200 million.

Company management noted with pride that several years back the company had started selling into the United States. The United States is a tough market, highly competitive as well as expensive for an SME, but the firm was slowly winning orders, focusing on the northern-tier border region and avoiding a full-blown effort. Still, U.S. orders now accounted for just over 10 percent of total sales and were inching up. The company took a bit of satisfaction in having proven that it could go toe-to-toe with any of the American competitors; all it lacked was the resources for a national campaign. The company was gradually building out its sales in the United States when Korea "happened."

What happened was an out-of-the-blue order—by fax—for US$10,000 worth of equipment. This was a nice order, especially considering no one remembers any dealings with the customer, but these things occasionally happened. What was more interesting was that similar orders came in almost monthly, and soon the company was selling over US$100,000 annually in Korea. Not a lot in the greater scheme of things, but it was enough to make Korea the company's third largest market, after Canada and the United States.

Also, if US$100,000 was coming in with no work, what kind of results would there be if the company actually made a sales effort in Korea? There had to be at least a million dollars' worth of business there. In fact, a quick look at some economic statistics showed that the Korean economy was one-seventh the size of the American economy, so the CEO reasoned that even with a modest effort he should be able to hit around US$3 million in sales—one-seventh of what he currently sells in the United States. Not a bad start.

So the company did what it did in America and in Canada: sent a small sales team to Korea to call on the large bathroom fixture companies, other household goods distributors, plumbing supply firms, and the like.

Six months into the Korean experiment, there were no orders, or no orders beyond the original faxed orders. Frustration set in at the company head office. Tempers flared. Criticism flew. Finally, the CEO let go with an outburst, asking if Koreans used their bathrooms differently.

Three months later, the company wound up its Korean operations, let go of its sales team, threw out its Korean language material. No sales had been recorded, and the company had sunk almost a half million dollars into the effort.

Why Should You Study Competitors?

Why is it important to study the competition well before taking the plunge into a new foreign market? Before answering this question, it is worth defining what we mean by competitors. In our view, you ought to view competitors in the context of the specific customers you'll target in a foreign market. This suggests an important do and don't: **Do** focus on competitors whose weaknesses you might be able to exploit as you seek to take market share in the foreign market, and **don't** study competitors in a foreign market with an eye toward creating a me-too strategy.

You should also recognize that what is a mass market product at home may initially be a niche product in a foreign market. For example, when McDonald's entered China, it initially offered a high-end experience, meaning that only affluent Chinese could go to a restaurant or would experiment with foreign cuisine. When Nissan introduced Datsun into the United States in the 1960s, it initially distributed the product only on the West Coast.

You should study the competition in a foreign market because the resulting insights will help you decide whether you can gain enough market share to make the foreign foray worthwhile. What kinds of insights could possibly make such research worthwhile?

Such research can provide two basic perspectives:

1. **Customer View.** As we discussed in Chapter Four, it is imperative that you understand what customers want and make sure that your company can give those customers a better value proposition. But in our view, your company is likely to do better going into a foreign market if it appeals to customers in a new way than if it goes after the customers that incumbent competitors already serve. For example, in the 1990s, Ryanair had enormous success opening a half-price shuttle service between Dublin and London because it was offering an alternative to customers who had previously taken a nine-hour ferry ride between the two countries, rather than going head-to-head for British Air's business customers. To discover such opportunities, we advise you to map out the different customer groups in the foreign market and distinguish between the crowded space and the open opportunities.
2. **Activity View.** Studying competitors can also yield useful insights into what it takes to compete in the foreign market.

Specifically, by studying the way incumbent competitors perform critical activities—such as distribution, customer financing, manufacturing, marketing, sales, and addressing regulatory requirements—you can learn more about what you would need to do in order to compete successfully. In the case of Ryanair, it offered a much lower priced service on a single type of inexpensive aircraft, and it located itself in airports with relatively low landing fees. To discover how competitors perform critical activities needed to satisfy customer needs, you should study competitors' value chains and compare them with your own to gain insights into what it takes to compete.

The purpose of this chapter is to help you answer two fundamental questions regarding competitors:

1. Can your company occupy a position in the foreign market that will offer enough potential customers a competitively distinct product?
2. Can your company perform the critical activities needed to occupy that position profitably?

In this chapter we take a close look at the first question and kick off an examination of the answer to the second one that will extend through Chapters Six and Seven.

To address the first question, you need to map out the market and distinguish its crowded and unoccupied spaces. For the crowded space, you need to assess whether you can offer a product that is so much better that customers will switch from incumbents. For the unoccupied space, you need to figure out whether it's unoccupied because it lacks profit potential or because it is an untapped opportunity.

To make these determinations, you should weigh the following issues:

• **Market segments.** Who are the customers for the product in the foreign market? More specifically, who are the direct customers—possibly distributors or wholesalers—and who are the downstream customers? Are there different segments of customers—for example, customers with common ways of purchasing and financing the product, and those with shared needs, such as price, quick delivery, and responsive service? If so, what are the five to ten most significant customer segments? How big and how rapidly growing are these segments?

• **Competitor positions.** Of these segments, which are occupied by incumbent competitors and which are unoccupied? For the occupied segments, how is the share distributed among existing competitors? Going back to insights gained from following the prescriptions in Chapter Four, what are the ranked needs of customers, and how well do customers perceive that the competitors in the segment satisfy those needs?

• **Unmet customer needs.** In both the occupied and unoccupied customer segments, are there specific unmet needs—such as for a half-price product or for a product that is uniquely designed for each customer—that would be worth satisfying? If so, could your company meet those needs better than incumbent competitors could? If your company could meet those needs, how difficult would it be for competitors to match or surpass your company's product?

To address the second question about competitor positions, you need to map out the value chains of the incumbent competitors in the foreign market. This means getting a detailed understanding of how the competitors perform critical activities—distribution, service, manufacturing, sales, and so on. You should also focus most intensely on the competitors with the largest share of the foreign market whose businesses are growing and contrast leaders' value chains with those of less successful competitors. Moreover, you should map out your own value chains and compare them to competitors'.

To get such answers, you should consider the following issues:

• **Leaders and laggards.** Which competitors have a large market share and are growing? Which ones have a big share but are losing share? Which small competitors, if any, are growing faster than the industry and taking market share from the leaders?

• **Value chain.** How do all these different groups of competitors perform the critical activities required to operate in the market? What are the key differences in the value chains of the leaders and laggards? How do these differences help explain why the leaders are gaining share while the laggards are losing it?

• **Strategic audit.** How does your value chain compare to those of the leaders and laggards? If your value chain is more like that of the laggards, is there any hope for your company to improve it? If so, how? If your value chain is more like that of the leaders, does this offer hope for your ability to compete in the new market? Or is your business more of a me-too? If so, is there a way for you to change your company's value chain so it will offer customers something uniquely valuable to them?

Chapter Six will examine in greater depth what this means for your company as you consider how to configure your value chains for the segments they target. And Chapter Seven looks at how to pick partners if you find you can't do it all yourself.

Key Research Findings on These Issues

In the cases we examine later in this chapter, we will present the nuances that lead to the following key findings on these three issues:

1. **Leaders and laggards.** The cases we'll soon discuss reveal that export leaders know their customers better than their competitors do. More specifically, the leaders understand the ranked criteria that customers use to decide which product to buy. In fact, these leaders are able to create a unique brand that attracts customers in different countries who are attracted to the primary premise of that brand.

2. **Value chain.** We also examine how leaders perform critical activities—such as product design, manufacturing, logistics, and marketing—in a way that supports that brand. Of course, to sustain a lead in export markets, companies must build a value chain that is difficult for competitors to copy as they try to regain lost market share.
3. **Strategic audit.** Finally, our cases reveal the importance of knowing, objectively, how good your value chain is relative to your competitors'. And they show that ongoing pressure to improve through objective feedback is critical to sustaining market leadership.

Competitor Case Studies

We examine how to analyze your competitors in a foreign market by looking at four case studies:

1. **French Gourmet,** a Hawaiian dough maker, exported to Asia and found that by focusing on how it could convince customers of its product quality and investing in further enhancing that quality, it could fend off competitors who tried to take away its lead.
2. **WATG,** a Hawaiian architectural design firm, now gets the vast majority of its work from clients outside the United States. It was able to gain market share—particularly in Asia—because customers in the hotel industry there perceived that WATG offered more specific hotel-related expertise than competitors in those countries, whose capabilities were more diffused.
3. **IKEA,** a global furniture retailer, has expanded its concept into many foreign markets because it has created a brand that attracts a meaningful segment of consumers in different countries around the world. It stays ahead of competitors by cutting prices on products that are beautifully designed to meet the specific tastes of consumers in different markets while maintaining an overall aura of coolness.
4. **Sosro,** an Indonesian bottled tea company, fended off global competitors Coca-Cola and Pepsi through its superior

knowledge of local tastes. It sustained a 70-percent market share despite the global giants' onslaught by coming up with new products that better met local needs.

French Gourmet

In 1994 Patrick Novak, CEO of French Gourmet, a Hawaiian dough company, decided that his company's growth had maxed out in the United States and it was time to export his product. Novak had started French Gourmet in 1984, supplying frozen dough to customers in Hawaii that operated high-end hotels, cruise lines, and restaurants.[1]

As the company began considering markets as far away as Singapore and Dubai, it discovered that it would need to do things differently in foreign markets. One key factor contributing to French Gourmet's success was the insight it gained into how potential customers perceived competitor offerings. The company learned enough about how those competitors operated to stay one step ahead of them as they tried to imitate its products.

Novak knew that the market in Hawaii was limited, and he envisioned a better growth opportunity from going global. "The market is very small here in Hawaii," he explained. "All you do is spin your wheels after a while. Spending a lot of time and money and energy for the next incremental growth is not worth it when you can do the same thing and capture a huge share of the market in Asia or on the U.S. continent."

Novak brought a global sensibility to the challenge of exporting his product. He had been an executive chef and received culinary training in France, where he was born. His initial foray was to export his French Gourmet Artisan Frozen Dough to Guam, Hong Kong, and Singapore.

He found that food-service customers there were more than willing to pay a higher price for quality products.

It is important to point out that Novak's first move was not to study his competitors in those foreign markets. Instead, he focused his attention on meeting with potential customers, understanding their needs, and recognizing that their perception of frozen dough was inconsistent with their desire for high quality.

Fortunately, Novak was able to overcome that perception by explaining to them that frozen dough is not baked; rather, "it's raw dough that is still baked fresh." Novak clinched his initial contracts by visiting hotels in these countries and conducting baking demonstrations using on-site ovens. Novak concluded that the quality of the product was so high that these demonstrations enabled him to gain a market foothold, noting, "The product speaks for itself."

Novak enjoyed a first-to-market advantage in frozen dough. His company was the first foreign frozen dough maker to export to Hong Kong and Singapore and his success naturally attracted competitors. And then, he says, "Asia started to open up for us in a very big way."

But that opening led six competitors to try to take away French Gourmet's market share. And those competitors attempted to compete on price. Rather than try to block these competitors by lowering its prices, French Gourmet focused its attention on boosting its product quality—improving its croissants, Danish, puff pastries, breads, and muffins—while maintaining its premium prices. Anchoring strategy to outperforming competitors on quality turned out to be a wise move. Novak pointed out, "Ultimately, it's the quality, and nobody could beat us. The [competitors'] price may be cheaper, but we stood our ground. Quality is paramount in Asia."

(Continued)

French Gourmet (*Continued*)

French Gourmet has set up operations around the world. As of 2010 it had eighty workers and a warehouse in Los Angeles. Seventy percent of its sales were from exports generated through a network of sixty-three food-service distributors on the U.S. mainland and in Guam, Hong Kong, Singapore, South Korea, Canada, and Dubai. Moreover, French Gourmet hopes to expand to Malaysia, Indonesia, Taiwan, and the Middle East.

Novak attributes the company's survival to his decision to go global and stay ahead of his competition there. With the cost of doing business in Hawaii rising—notably high shipping costs, particularly between California and Hawaii—he says that if French Gourmet had not gone into exporting, "I would be working much harder, making less income, and supporting a lot fewer local employees."

The French Gourmet case offers four lessons about competitors that can help SMEs considering global expansion:

1. Pick the right market segment. French Gourmet did an excellent job of finding a group of customers—or market segment—that was looking for a higher-quality product and willing to pay a price premium to get it. When exporting, make sure there are enough people in the new country who fit the market segment profile of the segment that buys your product in your home market.

2. Obsess over giving customers superior value. When entering a foreign market, you should be obsessed with finding customers for your product and meeting with them to understand what they want. And you should make sure that your product can satisfy those customer needs better than competitors'. Novak demonstrated his ability to overcome customer's misperception that frozen dough was of poor quality by hosting demonstrations at high-end hotels in Hong Kong and Singapore. French Gourmet essentially created a new market in these countries because the customers realized that its frozen dough better met their quality requirements.

3. Know whether competitors can take share. If you are successful in a foreign market, you are going to attract competitors—that's an essential feature of a free market. The key question is how hard it will be for competitors to take away your customers. You need to know how such competitors will attempt to do that. Novak saw that competitors thought they could win customers through price cutting. And that might have worked if the competitors were able to offer lower prices for products of similar or better quality. If French Gourmet's customers had cared more about price than quality, then Novak would have been in trouble. But because they cared more about quality, French Gourmet was able to fend off competitors who couldn't deliver products of similar high quality.

4. Invest in product attributes that will keep you a step ahead of the competition. The key to maintaining and growing your foreign market share is figuring out how to stay ahead of competitors. The key to achieving that is to look at the industry from the customer's perspective. If the customer buys on quality, then you need to make sure your product quality is better than that of all the other competitors. And if the customer cares about getting decent quality at the lowest price, you need to lower your costs below those of competitors. Again, Novak realized that customers cared about quality, so he stayed ahead of the competition by improving his products.

Wimberly Allison Tong & Goo (WATG)

> We determined early on that you have to be two
> things to do work around the world: nimble enough
> to go where the action is, and humble enough to
> listen once you get there.
> —*Howard Wolff, senior VP, WATG*

While the French Gourmet example demonstrates the
benefits of understanding a competitor's strategy vis-à-vis
the needs of customers in a foreign market, there are
other important competitor-related lessons. Among these:
if you're going into a foreign country, it is important to
analyze the capabilities of potential competitors in those
markets.

Understanding foreign market competitors' capabilities
can help you decide whether you have something unique
to offer customers there. A key factor for success in a
foreign market is that when a potential customer considers
your firm's capabilities in comparison to those of competing companies, your firm comes out on top. If your firm
can offer customers a better bundle of capabilities, then
not only will you be able to win new business, but it will
be difficult for competitors in those foreign markets to
take away your customers.

The global expansion of design firm Wimberly Allison
Tong & Goo, now known as WATG, is a case in point.
Howard Wolff, WATG senior VP, related the expansion story
to Peter Cohan.[2] George "Pete" Wimberly had founded
the Honolulu-based firm in 1945. Following its first design
project in 1945—renovation of the Royal Hawaiian Hotel
in Waikiki—Wimberly made an early decision to special-
ize in hospitality design. That one project helped to create the
firm's reputation and the demand for its expertise.

WATG took advantage of the postwar boom in hotel and resort development in the Pacific, at first by providing architectural services, and later expanding to include strategic consulting, master planning, landscape architecture, and interior design. By 2010, WATG had over three hundred people providing services worldwide from six offices around the globe. WATG does more work outside of its home country than any other U.S.–based architecture and design firm. In 2010, 93 percent of WATG's revenue came from outside the United States.

As early as the 1950s, WATG was doing work in the Asia-Pacific region. WATG aligned itself with the travel and tourism industry and, more specifically, followed the expansion of Pan American World Airways into the Pacific. WATG believed that travelers would seek a different hotel experience in Tahiti than they would in Toledo, and it set a goal of designing destinations with a unique sense of place. Its first such projects outside of Hawaii were in American Samoa, Pago Pago, and French Polynesia.

WATG thought it would be able to win business there because it believed that the hotel design expertise that it offered was not available in these locations. In each case, however, WATG partnered with a local architect who was familiar with the customs and codes of that locale. Howard Wolff said, "We determined early on that you have to be two things to do work around the world: nimble enough to go where the action is, and humble enough to listen once you get there."

Following its first completed international project—Hotel Tahiti, which opened in 1958—WATG designed Hotel Bora Bora, which debuted in 1960. Throughout the 1960s WATG worked in the South Pacific and in the 1970s expanded into Asia with projects like the Shangri-La Garden Wing in Singapore. In the 1980s WATG did

(*Continued*)

Wimberly Allison Tong & Goo *(WATG)* *(Continued)*

work in Australia and New Zealand, as well as Malaysia, Indonesia, Thailand, the Philippines, and Japan. In the 1990s, it expanded into Latin America, Europe, Africa, and the Middle East. By 2010, WATG had done work in 160 countries on six continents.

WATG has adapted to the changing needs of its clients. According to Wolff, "Our clients are getting quite sophisticated. Today, we find that titles are less important to them than they once were. They want to meet our design team and are less interested in having us send the president or chairman. Our Asian clients—and this is true around the world—now want to know who will work on their project. They want knowledge, expertise, creativity, and connectivity."

Two industry-specific changes have altered the way WATG works: technology and client concerns about the environment. Wolff explained, "Technology has enabled us to share work between offices effectively. In some cases, due to time zone differences, we are literally able to work around the clock to meet tight deadlines and get a client's project opened ahead of schedule."

Clients have caught up with WATG's concern with the environment. Wolff argued, "Environmental sensitivity has been a core value of WATG's for decades. We are delighted that clients are now embracing it, as well. We have not seen a diminishment of interest in sustainable design during the recession. On the contrary, owners see that going green not only is the right thing to do for the planet but also makes sense in terms of return on investment."

A key to WATG's export success has been getting to know the culture of each new country where it competes. According to Wolff, "We realize that imposing ideas from the outside doesn't work. Instead, we immerse ourselves in the culture of a specific place, looking and listening for time-tested answers to particular questions regarding appropriate design. Often we are able to provide a contemporary twist to a traditional design aesthetic, while making sure that how the building functions is just as important as how it looks."

As with any business, it helps to have clients who are willing to act as references. Wolff said, "We have taken advantage of our worldwide reputation and third-party endorsements. It helps to have people say nice things about us. Four out of five current projects are with repeat clients or were secured through referrals by repeat clients."

Not all of its export strategies have worked. For example, associating with universities did not pay off. Wolff explained, "One of our partners was teaching at the University of Hawaii, and we thought that leveraging his reputation would gain us exposure in collaboration with other academic institutions in places like China. The arena proved to be too academic and did not have much influence in the private sector. We tried it for about a year. The effort generated relationships but little return on investment dollars."

WATG also learned that gaining export market share through design competitions yields uneven results. Wolff said, "Design competitions are a mixed bag. In some cases, even the winning firm does not receive a commission. We have found that in many countries developers use competitions to get some good ideas at a nominal cost and/or to generate interest in their project by showing how many high-profile firms are willing to compete for the design. Many times the sponsor does not have project financing or even the means to reward the design firm for their efforts. We always try to talk a client out of a competition."

(Continued)

Wimberly Allison Tong & Goo *(WATG)* *(Continued)*

Moreover, WATG has its share of international failures. For example, it was too early to get into China. However, its capabilities in hotel and resort design ultimately enabled it to offer customers there a competitively unique set of capabilities. According to Wolff, "You can waste time and money by being too early in a location. For example, we were showing work in China in the early 1970s that never got built and we were never paid for. There was a lot of interest but not a lot of ability to make things happen back then. We decided to wait until they got their act together in terms of private-sector development, and now our work in China is 40 percent of our business worldwide."

WATG's export success springs from its focus on a specific market segment and applying its expertise to its clients' growth strategies. According to Wolff, "In the course of WATG's history and throughout the recent downturn, we have remained focused on serving the hospitality industry and exporting specialized expertise. While we remain a niche firm, we have carved that niche with a bulldozer ... adding services, expanding to new locations, and designing closely related building types (including retail, dining and entertainment facilities, theatres and performing arts centers, conference and convention centers, resort and urban residential communities, casinos, spas, and assisted-living facilities, for example)."

WATG offers six pieces of advice for first-time exporters:

1. **First, you've got to have something distinctive.** Otherwise, you'll waste a lot of money and find yourself competing solely on the basis of fee. There is no way that a U.S. firm can win at being the low-cost provider.

2. **Focus your energy and your resources.** No matter how big your company, you can't be everywhere. Do your homework, and invest strategically.

3. **Develop strong relationships with trusted advisors.** Follow existing clients into new geographic areas. Let them pave the way for you.

4. **Get on an airplane—often.** You can't expect to develop relationships or build a business by making one trip or even a handful. WATG has several people who spend 50 percent of their time away from home.

5. **Build a diverse team.** Having a multicultural, multilingual staff can help you enter new geographic territories while minimizing your risk.

6. **Determine whether to open an office, once you've done your homework.** Models for success include moving someone with seniority, moving someone with local knowledge, hiring locally, associating with a firm, and/or acquiring a firm. (WATG has employed a combination of all five of these strategies.)

IKEA

Imagine you're CEO of a retailer that's big in Sweden and decides to go after a position in the world's biggest market—America. You know the market is chock full of competitors, ranging from ones that offer the highest quality and exorbitant prices down to ones that sell far lower-quality versions of the same product category at the lowest possible price. As you consider setting up stores and building logistics networks, you realize that competing in America will be expensive. In such a crowded market, how will

(Continued)

IKEA (*Continued*)

you find a niche that's big enough to justify the investment and risk?

One way to do this is to create a state of mind that transcends national boundaries. Such a state of mind can draw people from all countries who share that vision. Moreover, if that experience is a unique one, enough people in each country share it, and your company serves like-minded people around the world better than any competitor, then your company has a good shot at making a profit when it goes into a big market like America.

This may sound very abstract and hard to pull off, but Swedish retailer IKEA has done it. IKEA has created a state of mind called IKEA World—a consumer experience that is satisfied through products with contemporary design, low prices, unusual promotions, and tremendous institutional enthusiasm. According to *Businessweek*, "IKEA provides a one-stop sanctuary for coolness. It is a trusted safe zone that people can enter and immediately be part of a like-minded cost/design/environmentally-sensitive global tribe. There are other would-be curators around—Starbucks and Virgin do a good job—but IKEA does it best."[3]

IKEA does not attract forceful competitive responses when it enters a new market because its share of the furniture markets in which it operates is fairly small, usually between 5 and 10 percent. However, a key element of IKEA's ability to compete in these markets against many different competitors is the power of that state of mind—as manifested in its brand. According to IKEA CEO Anders Dahlvig, "[A]wareness of our brand is much bigger than the size of our company." IKEA's brand makes it more than just a furniture store—it represents "a lifestyle that customers around the world embrace as a signal that they've arrived, that they have good taste and recognize value."

IKEA was founded by Ingvar Kamprad in 1943 when he was just seventeen. That's the year he began selling pens, Christmas cards, and seeds from a shed on his family's farm in southern Sweden. In 1951, IKEA's first catalog appeared, written entirely by Kamprad (a task he retained until 1963). IKEA's values are reflected in his 1976 pamphlet, *A Furniture Dealer's Testament*. Its aphorisms include "divide your life into 10-minute units and sacrifice as few as possible in meaningless activity"; "wasting resources is a mortal sin"; and "it is our duty to expand."

And when it comes to expansion, IKEA has surpassed other big retailers with its global success. For example, Walmart stores stumbled in Brazil, Germany, and Japan. France's Carrefour has yet to gain a foothold in the United States. As of 2005, IKEA had 226 stores in Europe, Asia, Australia, and the United States that were doing well and attracting 410 million shoppers a year. When IKEA opened a store in Jeddah, Saudi Arabia in September, 2004, thousands showed up for store vouchers and two people died in the crush. In London six thousand thronged to a February 2005 opening before police were summoned.

IKEA is growing fast and is more profitable than competitors. For the fiscal year ended August 31, 2005, its revenues rose 15 percent, to US$17.7 billion. And a Swedish analyst estimated that IKEA's operating profits for that year totaled US$1.7 billion (the company is privately held and does not disclose these figures). What is most interesting about this is that IKEA's 10-percent operating margins beat those of U.S. competitors like Pier I Imports (5 percent) and Target (7.7 percent) even as IKEA steadily cuts prices. IKEA achieves this growth in part by opening new stores at a clip of nineteen a year for 2006 (at US$66 million a store). In the United States

(*Continued*)

IKEA (*Continued*)

it opened its first store in 2000, opened five more in 2005, and by the end of 2010 had thirty-seven U.S. stores in operation.[4]

There are four keys to IKEA's success:

1. **Providing a unique customer experience.** The stores are similar around the world: blue-and-yellow buildings of about three hundred thousand square feet selling seven thousand different items. Parents can drop their kids off at a playroom so they can focus on walking through the store, catalogs in hand. There's a restaurant where shoppers can reenergize themselves. And when consumers have selected everything they want to buy, they pick up their purchases in flat boxes in the warehouse area, load them into their vehicles, retrieve their children, and drive home, where they assemble their purchases.

2. **Keep prices lower than competitors'.** IKEA is intensely focused on beating its competitors through lower costs and prices. In its headquarters in Helsingborg, Sweden, "a massive bulletin board tracks weekly sales growth, names the best-performing country markets, and identifies the best-selling furniture." IKEA also has visual reminders of the importance of cutting prices—in the entry to that headquarters building is a row of its popular Klippan sofas with models from 1999 to 2006, showing price drops from US$354 in 1999 to US$202 in 2006. IKEA's cost-cutting is focused on its regional U.S. competitors. While it generally tries to lower prices 2 percent to 3 percent each year, it cuts more when it wants to attack rivals in certain segments. Mark McCaslin, manager of IKEA Long Island, in Hicksville, New York, said, "We look at the competition, take their price, and then slash it in half."

3. **Designing products tailored to each market's tastes.** IKEA's unique skill is finding ways to offer designs that each market will want because of both their beauty and low price. Josephine Rydberg-Dumont, president of IKEA Sweden, said, "Designing beautiful-but-expensive products is easy. Designing beautiful products that are inexpensive and functional is a huge challenge." To overcome the challenge, in 2005 IKEA's twelve full-time designers and eighty freelancers worked with IKEA's production teams to pick materials and the least expensive suppliers. For example, in China, to commemorate the year of the rooster, IKEA produced 250,000 plastic placemats—which sold out in three weeks.

4. **Building an efficient global supply chain.** As of 2011, IKEA had two thousand suppliers in fifty countries.[5] It uses creative approaches to match suppliers with products. For example, it once used ski makers—experts in bent wood—to manufacture its Poang armchairs. These relationships are similarly focused on cost cutting. When it asked designers to find innovative uses for discarded and unusual materials, for example, they came up with a storage system made from recycled milk cartons.

These key success factors are particularly important to IKEA's efforts to compete in America. When it first entered the market in the early 1990s, IKEA failed to put many of them into practice, and it suffered tremendously as a result. According to Steen Kanter, former head of IKEA's U.S. operation, "We got our clocks cleaned in the early 1990s because we really didn't listen to the consumer." This inattention to customers took many forms. The U.S. stores were in poor locations and scrimped on floor space, and prices were too high. They failed to tailor European products to U.S. consumers; for example, offering beds

(*Continued*)

IKEA (*Continued*)

sized in centimeters rather than the expected twin, queen, and king sizes.

IKEA brought in a new manager who fixed the problems. The company adapted parts of its product line, chose new and bigger store locations, cut prices, and improved service. And it spent time studying the needs of specific segments of the U.S. market, having recognized that there are wide differences among them. For example, to reach California's Hispanic consumers, "designers visited the homes of Hispanic staff. They soon realized they had set up the store's displays all wrong. Large Hispanic families need dining tables and sofas that fit more than two people, the Swedish norm. They prefer bold colors to the more subdued Scandinavian palette and display tons of pictures in elaborate frames." To address this, IKEA's U.S. interior design director, Mats Nilsson, introduced warmer colors to the showrooms and added more seating and wall art.

IKEA continues to pay close attention to U.S. customers' preferences. Pernille Spiers-Lopez, head of IKEA North America, pointed out, "Americans want more comfortable sofas, higher-quality textiles, bigger glasses, more spacious entertainment units."

The IKEA case offers three important lessons about how to think about competitors when exporting to a foreign market:

1. **Understand what the consumer in a foreign market wants.** If you're thinking about exporting your product to another country, then you've probably achieved a certain level of success in the country where you started. The question you need to answer before going into a foreign market is whether there is an unmet customer need for your product in that new market. If you have a product

that's the same as what a competitor in that market already offers, then it will be hard for you to take market share. IKEA created a new global market based on an IKEA World state of mind. And it did a better job than any competitor at satisfying the needs of people with a preference for the "coolness" they perceived in IKEA products. If your product satisfies such an unmet need, you ought to be able to beat some of the competition in that foreign market.

2. **Make sure your value chain is consistent with your company's competitive positioning.** If you understand the unmet needs of customers in a foreign market, the next test you'll face is how to satisfy those needs consistently. Furthermore, if you can do what's required to meet that test, you must also stay ahead of competitors in that market who may look at your success and try to replicate it. To make your foreign market entry worthwhile, you'll need to sustain your lead in the face of fierce competitive pressure. IKEA built a global value chain that could sustain such pressure. Its design process, supply chain, store experience, and ever-lower prices helped it to stay ahead, because competitors were hard-pressed to do all these things well.

3. **Keep the pressure on yourself to stay ahead of the competition.** Business changes constantly; to keep pace with the change, you need to keep some powerful values in mind even as you challenge and reexamine your operating assumptions. In IKEA's case, this means tracking its competitors' prices and making sure that it cuts its prices to well below that level. But it also means getting to know the needs of customers in different markets and changing its strategies to do a better job than competitors in meeting those needs. A big lesson from IKEA is that even a successful exporter can stumble if it strays from such principles. Fortunately for IKEA, when it returned to its principles it was able to turn around its faltering business in America.

Sosro

If you're a successful small company, can you fend off a huge global competitor? And if so, can you use the strategies that enabled you to fend off that competitor to expand into new markets?

These questions come to mind in considering what happened to an Indonesian bottled tea company, Sosro, when U.S. giants Coca-Cola and Pepsi tried to take a share of its successful tea drinks business.[6]

Family-owned Sosro was the first bottled tea brand in Indonesia. It started making Teh Botol, a jasmine-flavored black tea drink, in the 1970s. A failed promotional effort planted the seed of its eventual success: at public tastings in the capital city of Jakarta, impatient customers had to wait too long for the fresh-brewed tea to chill. Sosro tried brewing the tea off site and delivering it to the market by truck, but travel over bad roads caused too much spillage along the way. The company decided to bottle the tea— and a winning product was born.

When Coca-Cola decided it wanted a share of Sosro's market, the soft-drink giant tried to attract Indonesian consumers with its Frestea brand. Pepsi entered the competition with its Tekita. But despite the competitive onslaught, Sosro has maintained 70 percent of the Indonesian noncarbonated drinks market.

Sosro kept ahead of competitors by introducing new products attuned to Indonesian tastes, just as these rivals tried to launch their new products. Sosro's superior knowledge of local tastes and its refusal to become complacent about its success have helped the company outsmart its global competitors.

Over the years, Sosro has introduced a variety of products whose raw materials are grown in Indonesia.

For example, Sosro's attractive bottle design is updated from time to time and it offers customers a range of packaging choices, from a returnable glass bottle to three sizes of Tetra Pak to a pouch. Sosro offers a fruit tea, Botol Kotak, and S-Tee. The company relies on local sources such as tea grower Gunung Slamet PT, named after an active volcano in Indonesia.

The big lesson of the Sosro case is that you can fend off global competitors if you know your customers better than your competitors do and you can satisfy those customers' needs more effectively than the competition. Sosro shows potential for exporting success; should it ever choose to, it could apply its deep insights into Indonesian tastes to exporting its products to other countries with significant Indonesian populations.

Gaining the Competitor Knowledge to Take Overseas Market Share

So how can you gain the knowledge of competitors that you need to take market share in a foreign market? Here's a three-step methodology to consider:

1. **Find out what local competitors do to satisfy those needs, if anything.** If you're lucky enough to find customers with unmet needs, you need to learn more about those competitors. Specifically, you need to find out about competitors' goals, strategies, capabilities, and assumptions about the market you're going to enter. You can do this by studying publicly available information about the competitors and by talking with their suppliers, customers, former employees, and local industry associations and consultants. Your goal is to

understand whether these competitors would have an easy time knocking down your efforts to take market share.

2. **Decide whether you can beat your competitors.** Once you've learned about these competitors' strengths and weaknesses, you need to figure out how your company stacks up. Specifically, assess whether you can do a better job of satisfying those unmet customer needs than competitors. If you can, then that knowledge will help you to forge your strategy to take share in the new market. If not, then perhaps you should look elsewhere.

3. **Evaluate whether you'll be able to stay ahead of competitors if they decide to copy your strategy.** Finally, you need to figure out how easy or difficult it will be for competitors to copy what you're doing in the foreign market. The competitor research just outlined should give you the knowledge to answer that question. If competitors are locked into a way of operating that would make it hard for them to copy your strategy, that would be good news. On the other hand, if it would be easy for competitors to copy what you've done, then you need to figure out how you can do something to stay a beat ahead of the local competition.

Lessons for Fixture Corp.

What lessons could plumbing supplier Fixture Corp. have learned from its failed foray into Korea?

1. **It failed to learn the market realities in Korea.** The core problem was that the initial unsolicited Korean orders came from an international hotel chain. There was no real Korean order. The Korean plumbing market is considered closed, with only a few suppliers in close relations with distributors. There is no opportunity to break in the way a company can in Canada and the United States. The Canadian company had encountered some false positives and drawn broad general conclusions about the market from some relatively small orders.

2. **It lacked the skills to go global.** Fixture Corp.'s international expertise was quite limited—indeed, almost nonexistent. Its success in the U.S. market probably attests more to the quality of its product and its proximity to the United States then to any international marketing acumen. It should indeed be proud of its success in the United States, but it should not conclude from this success that it enjoyed an understanding of exporting or of more distant markets.

3. **It did not prioritize.** Fixture Corp. did not play to its strength. It would have been better if it had invested in building out a U.S. sales force rather than going to Korea.

Competitor Knowledge Checklist

Do you know enough about competitors to gain and keep market share in a foreign market? Break down your domestic market by market share of the largest companies. Now break down your target market in the same fashion. What are the main differences in competitive behavior between these markets? Is it a more consolidated or a fragmented market? Does

Questions	Answers (Yes or No)
Have you met with potential customers to find out whether they have unmet needs that your product could satisfy?	
Have you determined how to evaluate whether local competitors would be able to copy your product easily?	
Do you know these competitors' goals, strategies, capabilities, and assumptions?	
Can your company do a better job than competitors at satisfying unmet customer needs?	
Can your company sustain its lead against these competitors' efforts to reverse your market share gains?	

competition shape up according to geographical lines, socio-economic status, ethnicity, or other factors?

Once you've completed this analysis, answer the following questions. If you can answer "Yes" to all five, chances are good your company can meet and beat the competition in a new foreign market.

Conclusion

Studying competitors can help you take your product into a foreign market. But doing so effectively depends on how you approach the task. The key is to avoid trying to imitate what competitors are doing in the foreign market. Mimicry is not a strategy. Instead, you need to find an unmet need in that foreign market and do a better job than competitors at satisfying the need. If you can keep from getting complacent—by coming up with new products that stay ahead of the competition—you boost your chances of getting a payoff from exporting your product.

Notes

1. Details of the French Gourmet case and all quotes are from Christie Wilson, "Growing by Going Global," *Hawaii Business*, August 2010 http://www.hawaiibusiness.com/SmallBiz/August-2010/ Growing-by-Going-Global/.
2. Howard Wolff, interview with Peter Cohan, December 15, 2010.
3. Unless otherwise noted, all information and quotes for this IKEA case study are from Kerry Capell and others, "IKEA: How the Swedish Retailer Became a Global Cult Brand," *Businessweek*, November 14, 2007, http://www.businessweek.com/magazine/content/05_46/b3959001 .htm.
4. "Number of IKEA Stores in the USA," *NumberOf.net*, April 27, 2010, http://www.numberof.net/number-of-ikea-stores-in-usa/.
5. "Where Are IKEA Products Manufactured?" IKEA web site, February 16, 2011, http://www.ikea.com/us/en/customerservices/faq.
6. The Sosro case study is based on Hopenow, "A Local Drink Beats Global Competition," Nowpublic.com, April 7, 2010, http://www .nowpublic.com/tech-biz/local-drink-beats-global-competition.

Chapter Six

CAPABILITIES:
WHAT YOU NEED TO WIN

K in Tok Meng was feeling a little better. He had been sweating through his move into Malaysia for almost two years, and he thought that he had—finally—solved his problems and gotten his business on the right track. But it took a good long period of trial and error before he could breathe easier, and the entire struggle was in one of the simplest product lines imaginable: automobile tires.

Kin Tok Meng owned and operated Tire Corp., a successful chain of tire retail shops in Singapore, with eight different locations and annual sales of over US$20 million. His father had started with a service garage in the 1950s, and over time his father and Kin had worked together to build out the locations. Approximately 75 percent of the revenue came from the sales of tires, with the remaining 25 percent coming from related service and parts sales and even the sale of gas at a station pump.

The business was still 100-percent family run, with Kin Tok Meng as the CEO and various cousins, nephews, and in-laws in different management and board positions. Business was good; the firm was well-respected, and there was no reason not to expand. However, given Singapore's relatively small population, an expansion at this point would mean going a few miles north into the neighboring country of Malaysia.

Two years previously, at a family business planning session, Kin Tok Meng had received the go-ahead to open up in Malaysia.

In the abstract, at least, this move made a great deal of sense. The ties between Malaysia and Singapore are friendly and close. There is an enormous amount of commercial and social interchange. Malaysians from the southern tip (the State of Johor) tend to be very familiar with Singapore and visit frequently to see friends or for shopping and entertainment. Although Malaysia has a lower per capita GDP than Singapore, this limitation is more than offset by two encouraging facts: Malaysia does not place high registration fees on car ownership as Singapore does, and Malaysia's population is significantly larger than Singapore's. Other successful Singapore retailers, from clothing to coffee shops had successfully expanded to Johor, so why not a tire shop?

So Kin Tok Meng opened up a Tire Corp. outlet in Johor. Establishing a store, stocking it, getting the government permits, training the staff was all relatively easy—not particularly different from doing the same in Singapore.

Kin also looked around Johor to get a sense of what retailing differences there might be compared with Singapore. One big difference was language. Singapore's official and dominant language is English, followed by Malay, Chinese (Mandarin), and Tamil. The lead language on Johor signs is Bahasa, the official language of Malaysia; English frequently appears in a secondary position. There is a smattering of Chinese as well. Kin redesigned the Tire Corp. signage to ensure that the text appeared first in Bahasa. He reduced the Chinese component to the company logo. And he kept the English prominent as well. Kin repeated this in redesigning the Internet site so that all material was now presented in English, Chinese, and Bahasa.

It was a successful launch.

Then Kin encountered his first lesson. Within a few months, with the store operating well and at a good location, sales were still only about 40 percent of equivalent store sales in Singapore. What could account for this sharp discrepancy in two very similar markets? Kin noticed that certain products were moving quickly and others were not moving at all. On examining the product mix of sales, Kin slapped his forehead with his palm. Of course. It was obvious.

What Kin saw was a customer preference in Malaysia for tires used for longer trips and highway driving, consistent with Malaysia's topography and modern highway system. This was different from Singapore's tightly controlled urban transportation system, in which high-speed driving was not the main use of the car. Kin quickly adjusted the product mix, offering a greater selection of tires designed for highway driving, and sales bubbled up.

Kin started spending one day a week in the Johor shop to get a better sense of the business, and this led to a second series of changes. Car ownership in Singapore was not as widespread as in Malaysia, due to registration fees; as a result, in Singapore cars tended to be more toward the luxury end, and in Malaysia, more toward the middle-market. Accordingly, Kin made further alterations to both pricing and marketing.

After eight months, sales had improved quite a bit. Kin's Johor shop was performing at about 70 percent of the level of his Singapore shop. The good news was that he had reached a break-even point. The bad news was that he still could not fully figure out why he was not doing better.

Malaysia was as car-crazy as any other country. It was prosperous and had a strong consumer culture. True, there was entrenched local competition, and differentiation in this industry is hard. However, for tire purchasers in Johor, his brand and his company would be just about as well known as the local shops.

What was missing? Kin got the answer at a Johor "kopitiam" (a local coffee house).

Sipping coffee one afternoon, Kin could not help but overhear the conversation at the next table, because it was somewhat boisterous. A group of Malaysians were discussing a cross-country road rally their group had just held. Like any group of sport enthusiasts, they were retelling tales of the race—the various adventures and close shaves.

These are my target customers, thought Kin. *These fellows love cars. They know the details and the performance specs.*

They are sophisticated customers. The kind of people our shop should embrace.

Then it dawned on him to check through customer details. He found the missing piece. About 70 percent of the customers in Johor were male, whereas in Singapore the customer base was closer to fifty-fifty. Kin adjusted his marketing again, and sales moved up again.

Now his Johor shop was running just 10 percent behind his Singapore shop. But reaching that point had taken almost two years of experimentation.

Capabilities as a Key Business Issue

In the previous two chapters we discussed why it's important for you to understand the needs of customers in foreign markets and how well competitors can meet those customers' needs. If you think you can do a better job than competitors at meeting those customers' needs, the challenge you need to overcome is to identify the *capabilities* you'll need to win over those customers. This requires three elements: diagnostic skills, learning skills, and self-awareness. We will discuss each in turn.

What do we mean by capabilities? They're the activities—such as product design, marketing, manufacturing, logistics, sales, and customer service—that you'll need to perform in order to meet customer needs better than competitors do. When we talk about capabilities, the key point to recognize is that all competitors in a foreign market have them. If you want to win, you'll have to perform these activities in a way that is different and better than the way competitors do them. Presumably you already do this—at least to some extent—in your home market (see Figure 6.1). However, the new market could have different capability requirements that might change the basis of competition (see Figure 6.2).

First, you need diagnostic skills. What are the components of success in the new market, and how might they differ from your home market? Which of your home market skills and strengths cannot be transported to the new market? These two

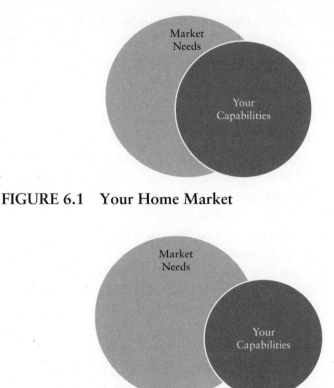

FIGURE 6.1   Your Home Market

FIGURE 6.2   Your New Market

questions reveal the capabilities gap that you need to bridge by replacing or rebuilding in your new market. Although all this may sound daunting, it doesn't have to be. If you take our advice and start your exporting strategy with a move into a market that's similar to the one you sell to now, then you may not need to change much. Specifically, you may be able to gain a reasonable share of a foreign market simply by partnering with the right distributor and continuing to do everything else—such as product design, manufacturing, and service—the same way you already do.

Second, you will need to become a learning organization. You might not fully evaluate the capability gap because you might not understand the need for a new capability until you decide to export your product. Kin Tok Meng learned many things with his Johor tire shop, but most important, he learned to learn. Gathering data, getting the facts on the ground, listening to customers, and then analyzing this material are all part of the challenge in the new market.

A learning organization gets feedback from its stakeholders—such as customers, employees, distributors, and suppliers—and uses that feedback to change the way it operates. The goal of a learning organization is to grow by adapting to the changing needs of its stakeholders. And a learning organization operates on an agnostic premise: the belief that its past assumptions may be helpful for it to compete in the future—or they may hinder its ability to adapt and thus ought to be tossed overboard if they no longer serve a useful purpose.

Why do you need to become a learning organization if you go into a foreign market? The reason is simple—despite your efforts to pick a country that's similar to the one where you got started, and despite your efforts at diagnosis, there will still be differences between the two markets. And since you don't know for sure ahead of time what those differences might be, it's better to assume that you'll have to maintain an open mind and keep looking for those differences. Business model flaws in a home market may be comfortably offset by strengths of familiarity and customer loyalty. However, equivalent short-comings in a new market could be fatal, as neither of these home market strengths exists.

Finally, regarding capabilities, you need a degree of self-knowledge. This means that you need to be aware that your home market business model probably includes strengths and weaknesses. There are elements of the business that might be world-class or that at least healthily beat the competition. However, there may also be elements of your current business that are not particularly strong or may not even be central to your business success. Do you need your own trucks, or can an outside firm handle delivery for you? Do you need to provide financing, or can a bank manage that better? The point is, your move into a new market allows you to reconfigure and reweight these elements of your business.

How can you make the right investments in capabilities so that your export strategy succeeds? To answer this question in the affirmative, we've found that it helps to address the following issues:

- Which of your core capabilities can help you compete in the export market?
- Which of those capabilities must you change if you want to gain export market share?
- Do you have a learning or evaluation mechanism that allows you to recognize whether you are closing the gap?

Key Research Findings on These Issues

Our research and the case studies that follow suggest that if you can answer those three questions you are well on your way to deploying the capabilities that your company needs to succeed in export markets. How so?

1. **Which of your core capabilities can help you compete in the export market?** Ideally, if you want to export your product, there should be end users of the product who are similar to each other even though they live and work in different countries. If that's the case, then even though you may need to distribute your products in different retailers for each country and you may employ different marketing channels to reach the consumers in those countries, you end up selling to the same kind of customer. In this chapter, we explore a few cases where this dichotomy is relevant. We urge you to go after export markets where your product development and other key capabilities will help you to gain share in that market. The key point is that if the similarities in your capabilities in different markets are greater than the differences, you can boost your chances of export success.
2. **Which of those capabilities must you change if you want to gain export market share?** The customers in the export market may have different needs than those in your home market.

And because of those different requirements, you may need different capabilities to satisfy the differing requirements. For example, if you manufacture and supply auto parts in the United Kingdom and decide to export them to Japan, you may need to open up a fully stocked warehouse next to your Japanese customer's plants. Why? Your UK customer may be satisfied with a six-hour delivery lag, but the Japanese customer requires delivery within thirty minutes.

3. **Do you have a learning or evaluation mechanism that allows you to recognize whether or not you are closing the gap?** You need to be able to methodically and regularly evaluate your business operations and the market response in your new market. Given your lack of history in this new market, you will have to devote disproportionate resources to this project. In which customer segments are you outperforming or underperforming? How do your warehouse operations compare to your home market operations? What about manufacturing or distribution? How do these features compare with your competitors in your new market? You will need to develop simple measurement tools to measure your progress. Kin Tok Meng took several approaches: He looked at his product sales. He listened to customers. And he adjusted product mix and adjusted again.

Capabilities Case Studies

We examine the challenge of self-knowledge by looking at three case studies:

1. **AHAVA**, a US$150 million (2009 revenue) Israeli cosmetics firm, has expanded into thirty countries since its 1988 founding. Four key capabilities have driven its export success: product development, marketing, distribution, and exclusive licensing of its scarce and valuable ingredients.

2. **Iscar helps Frontline Australasia win market share.** Frontline Australasia, a US$100 million (estimated 2010 sales) Australian auto parts maker, is able to win against Indian and Chinese

competitors who may have lower labor costs due to (1) its focus on customers who value precision and manufacturing quality, and (2) a partnership with Israel's Iscar, whose world-leading precision tools enable Frontline to make substantial profit margins on precision products by making them far more efficiently.

3. **Celeno,** a multimillion-dollar semiconductor company, decided to shift its export focus from the United States to China to take advantage of the higher economic growth rates. Thanks to a better product and an effective sales campaign, Celeno won a contract that could be worth US$50 million with a leading Chinese telecommunications company.

AHAVA

Imagine you are a small company with a product that sells well in your tiny home country. But if you have any ambitions for growth, you will need to find a way to sell that product in at least ten different countries. And in so doing, you may need to harness somewhat different skills. Specifically, you may need to change the product's formulation and packaging, meet different regulations, make different financing arrangements, and forge partnerships with different distributors. Could all the country-specific value chain tailoring be worthwhile?

For AHAVA, an Israeli cosmetics firm, the answer appears to be "Yes." AHAVA was founded in 1988 as a single stand selling bottles of body scrub to tourists. By 2009, AHAVA generated US$150 million in annual sales of moisturizers, scrubs, and beauty masks in thirty countries, and two-thirds of those sales were outside Israel. In the United States, its largest and most profitable market, AHAVA had distribution deals with Lord &

(Continued)

AHAVA (*Continued*)

Taylor, Nordstrom, and beauty-supply chain Ulta, and spent millions on advertising targeted at wooing American consumers.[1]

Ziva Gilad, a local spa technician, founded AHAVA after noticing tourists bottling Dead Sea mud to take home. Gilad and partners from four nearby kibbutzim (communal settlements) started selling plastic bottles of mud and salt crystals to Dead Sea tourists, later marketing them through stores across Israel. They generated US$1 million in 1988 revenue, but they also realized that AHAVA could grow further only if it began exporting. AHAVA CEO Yacov Ellis, who joined AHAVA in 2003, said, "The future of any cosmetics company can't be in Israel. There are only seven million people in this country."

To achieve its growth goals, AHAVA began to invest in its global capabilities. By the mid-1990s, AHAVA was exporting to Europe and the United States. However, it took until the early 2000s for AHAVA to invest in global marketing, advertising, and branding. In 2008 AHAVA's efforts to build these capabilities attracted a capital injection from Shamrock Holdings, a Disney-owned investment fund, which bought 20 percent of AHAVA.

Igal Litovsky, senior vice president at Shamrock and an AHAVA board member, is in charge of boosting AHAVA's U.S. market share. Litovsky's goal is for AHAVA to double or triple in size by 2013.

AHAVA has a collection of capabilities that give it a competitive advantage. For example, it's the only cosmetics company licensed by the Israeli government to mine raw materials at the Dead Sea. That makes AHAVA the sole source for competitors who want to use Dead Sea mud and salt. Between 2007 and 2009, AHAVA spent US$20 million on advertising and marketing. And in 2008 the company gained more control over its U.S. and Canadian distribution when it bought 50 percent of its exclusive U.S. distributor—now called AHAVA North America.

AHAVA also retails its products in a way that is consistent with its high-end brand. Although some competitors sell in mall stands, AHAVA products are available only in upscale chains such as Nordstrom in the United States and Sephora in France. As of 2009, AHAVA had flagship stores in Berlin, London, Singapore, and Israel and by 2014 expected to open similar shops in Los Angeles, Miami, and New York City. Capitalizing on the new popularity of mineral makeup, AHAVA planned to introduce its own line in 2010.

AHAVA also invests in the capabilities needed to satisfy consumers' need for natural ingredients in cosmetics. AHAVA purifies its own water and claims to use "minimally invasive techniques to harvest the mud and minerals used in its products." AHAVA does not test ingredients on animals, and its products are packaged in recyclable containers.

CEO Yacov Ellis offers many useful lessons for first-time exporters.[2] Here are five:

1. **Don't focus on the size of the target market. Focus on your strategy.** When a first-time exporter looks at the Chinese market, for example, it is tempting to see a billion potential consumers and decide to go after them. However, in Ellis's view, it is important to focus on your main markets. For AHAVA, this meant concentrating on developing a brand in the markets that were the most developed for premium cosmetics—such as the United States and Europe. Ellis pointed out that although these markets were difficult, success there would give AHAVA credibility when it came to establishing AHAVA's brand in the large Asian markets.

(Continued)

AHAVA (*Continued*)

2. Focus on the long-term value of export markets. If you're considering going into an export market, it is important to accept that it will take a long time to get a payoff. More specifically, Ellis notes that in AHAVA's case, it recognized that its efforts to export would not generate profits for at least three years. Although the time for a payoff is not likely to be the same for all industries, if you are not willing to wait years for a return on your export strategy, it may be a mistake to take the first step.

3. Bring in outside knowledge. Although it may not be true for all industries, in the case of cosmetics, AHAVA found that it was useful to hire people who could bring outside knowledge in order to achieve its export goals. Fortunately for the company, Ellis was able to recruit people with industry expertise who had previously worked in New York and subsequently decided to move to Israel.

4. Partner to augment your capabilities. Because coming up with new products that meet the needs of its consumers is critical to its brand, AHAVA found that it needed more effective R&D capabilities than it could afford. AHAVA's customers were women who wanted products that were made from natural ingredients, were safe, and had proven benefits for their skin. In order to obtain the R&D capabilities required to develop such products, AHAVA decided to partner with universities in the European Union whose researchers could help it develop effective skin care products.

5. Use your home base as a testing ground for new ideas. Given the competitive intensity of the cosmetics business, innovation is essential for AHAVA. This means that it needed to try out new ideas. But not all new ideas succeed, and therefore AHAVA needed a way to experiment frugally. To that end, AHAVA tests out its new product ideas in Israel. It is a small market, but if an idea works there, the company is confident that it will sell in its export markets. And if it does not work, the cost of the failure will be relatively modest. The general lesson is that it makes sense to use your home country to test out new ideas before exporting them.

To these lessons we add three more:

1. **Match your capabilities to your market.** As we illustrated earlier, it is critical for your company's capabilities to match the needs of your customers. That means that your product must meet their needs, you need to distribute that product in a retail store or other channel where they normally shop, and you have to communicate with them about the way that product meets their needs and draw them into the retail channel. AHAVA does this effectively in every country where it exports.

2. **Be prepared to invest in those capabilities to grow.** Of course setting up marketing and distribution for your product in a new country can be costly. As a small company, you'll want to make sure you do this in a way that does not require enormous financial resources. AHAVA seems to have done this—probably by dividing the revenues from the products it sells in different countries between itself and its retailers. Most likely, AHAVA's biggest export-related expense is its marketing. However, it has developed sufficient experience that it believes it can calibrate such spending profitably.

3. **Match your distribution and marketing to country-specific differences.** Each country has different distribution and marketing requirements. You'll distribute your product through different retailers in the different countries, and you'll advertise through different media. But to export

(*Continued*)

AHAVA (*Continued*)

effectively, you'll be trying to reach the same consumer in those different countries—otherwise, you'll probably be at a competitive disadvantage. AHAVA's strategy of opening up different export markets around the world suggests that it has figured this out.

Iscar Helps Frontline Australasia Win Market Share

One way to win new business is to help your customers compete more effectively in their markets by helping them lower their costs while boosting the quality of their product. If you can do this in countries around the world, you can build a global business in unexpected countries.

For example, Australia is generally thought of as a high-cost country when placed in a competitive bidding situation with China. But an Israeli company, Iscar, was able to export its machine tools to an Australian auto parts maker, Frontline Australasia, because Frontline was able to use Iscar machines to win a major client of its own in Australia: GM subsidiary VZ.[3]

Frontline's capabilities enabled it to emerge the winner out of twenty-one global bidders to supply exhaust manifolds for the VZ Commodore, a vehicle made by GM's Australian subsidiary. Frontline's win surprised GM headquarters executives; they expected an Australian winner to mean higher costs and therefore preclude a profit at their winning bid price. However, after six months of due diligence, GM concluded that Frontline could meet its needs better than competitors from other countries—and

Frontline CEO Kevin Hooper knew his company could earn a profit doing so.

Hooper pointed out that, following their winning GM bid, Frontline won work for other vehicles, including the VE Commodore and the VF. These competitive victories are powering a steady 25-percent to 30-percent annual growth rate for the company.

How did Frontline pull off this seeming contradiction of meeting exacting technical standards at the lowest price in the industry while also earning a hefty margin? Two critical management processes helped it achieve these results: lean manufacturing, a way of stripping an operation to peak efficiency, and picking suppliers who enable it to make its products to exacting standards while keeping costs low.

One such supplier is Iscar, whose cutting tools enabled Frontline to slash the time it takes to make its products by 25 percent to 30 percent. In so doing, Frontline can compete globally through its ability to provide world-class quality at a lower price than its peers. Hooper believes that by tapping into the intellectual capital of Iscar, Frontline can compete with companies from China and India that are typically considered to have much lower labor costs.

Nevertheless, Frontline opted out of the bidding for the supply of auto parts where price is the only factor that companies use to pick the winning supplier. Instead, Frontline maintained its focus on high-end, precision components that required "real know-how."

For those customers who value precision, Frontline's ability to compete depends on its use of the Iscar technology. According to Hooper, Iscar reduces Frontline's cycle times by at least 25 percent to 30 percent, enabling that area of Frontline's business to earn attractive margins. Hooper said,

(*Continued*)

Iscar Helps Frontline Australasia Win Market Share (*Continued*)

"In one particular drilling operation we were achieving 150 casting sets per drill, by using a new Iscar drill geometry we're now getting 3,500 casting sets per drill; efficiencies like that fall straight to the bottom line."

Frontline added to its precision-drilling capability when it inked its first contract with Iscar in 2003. Since then, Frontline has provided a test site for all of Iscar's new technologies. This gives Frontline a technological edge over competitors: access to the latest thinking from Iscar's R&D facility in Israel.

Iscar customizes its products to the needs of its customers. This has helped Frontline tremendously. An Iscar representative visits at least twice a week, and through their collaboration the two companies have been able to forge a close working relationship that helps them respond appropriately to each new set of circumstances.

Iscar has helped Frontline grow, and that aligns the two companies' economic interests in Australia. Hooper said, "Increasingly, we're looking for the same level of involvement that we have with Iscar from all of our suppliers. You could say that Frontline has become an Iscar convert; we're keen on their success in Australia, if only from a purely selfish point of view."

What lessons can business leaders take from the case? Here are two:

1. **Export products that create competitive advantage for your customers.** To win new business, you need to deliver a product or service that does a better job than competitors' of satisfying what customers want. This is just as true in your home market as it is when you go to export. Iscar wanted to export its machine tools to Australia, and in Frontline

it found a customer that could use its products to win new business. If you want to pitch your product to a customer in an export market, make sure that your product can deliver on that promise.

2. **Build that competitive advantage into product functionality and intellectual capital.** To deliver the winning edge to your customer in export markets, you can't rest on your laurels. You need to think as though there are competitors nipping at your heels—trying to copy your best ideas as quickly as they can. You must keep coming up with new ideas, so by the time your competitors have copied what you've done, their imitations are obsolete. That's why Iscar's R&D staff plays such an important role for its customers. Their willingness to help their best customers design new products to stay ahead of their competitors is a critical capability that helps them to gain and grow export market share.

Celeno

What if your company is used to exporting to the United States and Europe, but an economic jolt—such as the 2008 financial crisis—sucks all the economic oxygen out of your key markets? Do you close up shop and wait until things improve, or do you hop on an airplane and fly to the fastest-growing markets you can find for your products?

Israeli semiconductor startup Celeno Communications faced that choice when demand from Western telecommunications companies for its wireless digital TV technology evaporated. And instead of closing up shop, its top executives flew to China and ultimately won a major contract.[4]

(Continued)

Celeno (*Continued*)

Celeno's chips allow digital TV signals to be redistributed within a home using Wi-Fi wireless networking. After demand in the West slowed Celeno CEO Gilad Rozen tried to win business from Chinese telecommunications firms. The result was a July 2010 deal with Shanghai-based Shanghai Telecom and Wuhan-based FiberHome Telecommunication Technologies that could total US$50 million worth of chips. Rozen crowed: "China will become our largest market in 2011, accounting for 40 percent of our revenues. That compares with less than 10 percent [in 2010]."

This is a big shift in Celeno's global sales mix. In 2009, when Celeno launched commercial sales, it initially targeted U.S. and European telecommunications service providers for trials. Celeno signed up test carriers Stockholm's Stadsnät and Horizon Telecom of Chillicothe, Ohio. The result was "several million" dollars of 2010 revenues and "double-digit" millions forecast in 2011. In 2010, the United States and Europe accounted for 80 percent of Celeno sales.

Although Celeno's Western clients were pleased with its technology, the global economic slowdown delayed their rollout of new services that would use the chips. In response, Rozen and his executive team flew to the East frequently to meet with potential buyers there.

Celeno was attracted to the Chinese market for two important reasons. First, it is large and rapidly growing. Second, it is very interested in Celeno's area of expertise— IPTV—and eager to make a rapid decision about which vendor would supply the technology. Given China's decision-making speed, Celeno saw an opportunity to win a big contract quickly if it could meet the stringent technical requirements of its telecommunications companies.

Celeno's July 2010 deal with Shanghai Telecom would let the company roll out "triple-play" services offering voice, data, and digital TV in the Shanghai region. Shanghai Telecom hired systems integrator FiberHome Telecommunication Technologies to incorporate the Celeno chip into a set-top box.

Celeno's aggressive marketing campaign would have been worthless without a competitive product. But that product's superior performance won it the contract. According to Shihai Zhang, general manager at FiberHome, "We selected Celeno for its superior performance" such as the chip's ability to reject wireless interference. Celeno's technology was slated for installation in between two million and three million homes by 2013, with an average of two or three chips in each home.

And Celeno's technology is gaining a reputation as superior to that of competitors. Celeno believes that its technology is better because it addresses the limitations of existing wireless schemes. During Rozen's decade spent in an elite Israeli army intelligence unit, he helped create signal-processing technology to improve radar communication in hostile environments. Now Celeno has adapted this military technology for residential use. Rozen explains that the Celeno chip operates just like the radar tracking of an airplane—in this case, the object pinpointed is the end user's set-top box or boxes, and the chip can detect these through barriers such as walls and doors.

Celeno believes that it has some important lessons for first-time exporters. The company learned four key exporting lessons, detailed by Rozen:[5]

1. **Know export market product requirements.** You cannot win unless you're able to look at the product

(*Continued*)

Celeno (*Continued*)

requirements not from your perspective but from that of the potential export market customer. If the technical requirements of the export market are different from those in your home market, you will need to adapt.

2. Get a partner who understands the export market sales process. This is essential. Celeno did not understand the process in China, so it hired a well-connected Chinese sales representative who could help it win new customers.

3. Tap your investors to gain export market access. To gain that access, you may need to tap into the networks of your investors in that country. Celeno had a Chinese investor, Victor Tsao, who provided valuable introductions in China and helped it to jump start its China export strategy. Tsao gave Celeno instant credibility in China and helped identify the most relevant partners there.

4. Protect your export market cash flows. Make sure you are not putting your company in cash flow peril by hedging exchange rate risk and getting familiar with customer payment patterns so you can develop realistic export market cash flow forecasts.

We believe exporters should consider two additional lessons:

1. Understand the trade-offs between "easy markets" and "growth markets." This gets back to an issue we discussed earlier—if you have a choice of any country in the world in which to sell, where should it be? Earlier we recommended picking a market that is similar to the one where you currently operate. But if that market is going through economic turmoil, don't just sit there and hope it recovers. You may even need to get on an airplane and fly to a less familiar country where demand for your product is growing. The key to being able to do this successfully is having the capabilities that will make your product competitive in these faster-growing markets. Celeno clearly passed this test in China, and its success there is proof that you don't always need to export to a country that is very familiar to you. Celeno succeeded because its solution worked better for Shanghai Telecom than those offered by Celeno's competitors.

2. **Leverage capabilities across applications.** Can the skills that you've developed over the years in a different market help you compete in a new one? For Celeno, that answer was clearly "Yes!" Its CEO had worked for a decade in Israel's military, and he had the skills needed to build systems that could send and receive electronic signals across hostile boundaries. He applied those same skills to a different problem: sending TV signals through the walls and doors of a home so they could reach a variety of devices. If those skills are transferable—and they're world class—then customers in export markets around the world will clamor for them.

Building the Capabilities to Take Overseas Market Share

So what should executives do to get the capabilities they need to win in export markets? Here's a four-step methodology to use:

1. **Understand to what extent your strengths at home are strengths globally.** If you want to win in export markets, it's critical that whatever capabilities helped you win at home are valuable to customers overseas. If they are, then you'll be in a good position to apply those same strengths to the export markets. If not, as we'll see in Chapter Seven, you'll need to find a partner to close the capability gap.

2. **Start with like-minded customers in export markets.** As we saw in many of the cases we discussed earlier, you should use those capabilities to focus your selling efforts on customers in the export markets who have similar needs and demographic characteristics as your home-market customers. If you are selling to a similar kind of customer, then it's likely that your strengths in your home market will help you win sales in the export market. The key point is that you can boost your odds of winning in export markets if the experience you've accumulated in serving customers in your home market is helpful in gaining share in the export market.

3. **Tailor your export marketing strategy to target the same customers in the export markets.** To draw customers into the channels where you distribute your products in export markets (the selection of which we'll discuss in Chapter Seven), you need to create an effective export marketing strategy. If you are targeting the same kind of customer, this marketing strategy should be similar—but not identical—to the one in your home market. The differences should reflect an understanding of the cultural gaps between your home country and that of the export market. Simply put, your export marketing strategy should bring customers into your distribution channels without offending anyone unintentionally. If you are targeting the same kind of customer, then your marketing capabilities should help you attract new customers in the export market.

4. **Maintain a healthy paranoia to keep ahead of competitors nipping at your heels.** Although the second and third steps pertain mostly to companies that sell consumer products in export markets, this final step is important for all exporters. We believe that selling your product overseas demands a learning mindset. This means that you should set up listening posts in all the countries where you sell your products. These listening posts should feed you information about changing customer needs, new competitors, evolving regulations, and technological innovations that could be either threats or opportunities for your business. This can be as

simple as regular internet and blog searches. What are people saying about you and your products? And about your competitors? It can be as simple as having summer interns conduct consumer surveys or measure SKUs on shelves. And you should heed the insights that come from these listening posts and adapt your export strategy to make sure you can turn the changes into profitable opportunities rather than threats. Simply put, you can't rest on your laurels if you expect to gain share in export markets.

Lessons for Tire Corp.

Kin's tire story is illustrative of the central principles of this book.

First, he expands on taking the path of least resistance by going to the country he knows the best, and one with many cultural and linguistic similarities to his home market. Also of import, since it is very close, he can visit it regularly; in the early days he spends one day a week on site.

Second, he has enough wisdom and self-knowledge to know that he must make adjustments for culture and language, so he examines retail practices in his new market and makes appropriate adjustment to his signage and internet marketing.

Third, he is a learning organization (or at least a learning individual). He looks for feedback, and he is open to adjustment. Kin knows that despite his efforts, sales are weak, and he tries to find out why. By examining sales, he deduces that the preferred product mix is different, and that customer economics are different as well, despite the fact that the product is essentially identical to his offering in the home market.

Finally, he deduces different gender proportions among the customers, and he is able to refine his positioning and marketing even better.

Kin did not have a distinct capabilities gap, but he did have an experiential gap. He knew the tire business as well as anyone, and he knew Singapore retailing as well as anyone, but he had no particular background in Malaysian retailing. Fortunately,

Kin's desire to learn and his high degree of self-knowledge allowed him to adjust, learn, and adjust again.

Capabilities Checklist

Do you really have the capabilities to take a meaningful share of export markets? To answer that question in the affirmative, you should be able to answer "Yes" to all four of the following questions.

Questions	Answers (Yes or No)
Do you know which of your firm's core disciplines—product development, sales, marketing, manufacturing, and any others— you would outsource if you could reestablish your firm from scratch?	
Do you know whether your competitors keep all of these core activities in-house or use a different model?	
Have you decided whether to automatically reconstitute your home market business model in the new market? If you have decided not to are you open to experimentation?	
Are you capable of evaluating whether it makes sense to retain activities in-house or whether you need to look at another approach?	

Conclusion

You have a certain set of capabilities in your home market business that more or less matches your home market needs. However, your new market may require a different set or a different weighting of capabilities. Do not simply replicate your home market model in the new market.

Additionally, perhaps some of your home market capabilities were acquired over time for nonstrategic reasons and may add little value to your business (for example, you may have a collection of warehouses, but you are not in the warehouse business). Although it may admittedly be hard to extricate a business from existing relationships, the move into a new market will allow you to think through which capabilities you want to retain and which you want to let go.

Of course, lower pricing and similar attributes also serve to benefit the customer. If you can make, sell, deliver, and service your product effectively in that export market, then you can begin to build a viable position there. But to enhance and sustain that position, you'll need to build a learning organization that can adapt to changing conditions in export markets so you can continue to stay ahead of the competition there.

Notes

1. Case details for AHAVA are drawn from Peter Cohan's January 2011 interview with CEO Yacov Ellis, and from Michal Lev-Ram, "Turning Dead Sea Mud into Money," *Fortune*, December 10, 2009, http://money.cnn.com/2009/12/09/smallbusiness/AHAVA_dead_sea.fsb/index.htm.
2. Yacov Ellis, interview with Peter Cohan, January 6, 2011.
3. Frontline case details are drawn from Barbara Schulz, "Frontline Fronts Up to Global Competition," *Australian Manufacturing Technology*, May 2007, http://www.amtil.com.au/ UserFiles/File/05May%20lowres%20p80-82.pdf.
4. Celeno case details and quotes are drawn from Peter Cohan's December 2010 interview with CEO Gilad Rozen, and from Neal Sandler, "Israel's Celeno Finds Growth in the East," *Businessweek*, August 24, 2010, http://www.businessweek.com/print/globalbiz/content/aug2010/gb20100824_645830.htm.
5. Gilad Rozen, interview with Peter Cohan, December 20, 2010.

Chapter Seven

CAPABILITY GAP:
HOW TO CLOSE IT

Tim's Homemade Fudge had a business name that belied its substantial size and success. Starting in a home kitchen in Vancouver in 1980 (it really was homemade then), Tim soon opened up his first candy shop in downtown Vancouver, and over the course of a decade expanded to six shops in the greater metropolitan area. Then began the long march across Canada, until Tim's Fudge became a national chain of forty shops, each with a homey feel. Fudge and other confectionary products constituted about 60 percent of the firm's US$100 million annual revenue, with sandwiches, drinks, and other offerings making up the rest. Tim's wife worked at the company as CFO (she was a CPA), and their three children all had management jobs in the firm, having worked in the kitchens every summer during their school years.

By the 1990s, Tim had expanded modestly into the United States; he had five shops in the Pacific Northwest states of Oregon and Washington. They were close to Vancouver, and he could keep an eye on them. Tim was a bit ambivalent about expanding further in the United States, feeling that he could not afford the capital or management expertise to adequately compete in such a large market. He did not want to take on extra investors or dilute his ownership, nor did he franchise, so he had to finance growth largely out of earnings. He had a better feel for Canada, and he was comfortable with domestic expansion. Slow and steady, perhaps, but with low risk and within his comfort zone. Tim was proud that of the forty shops he had opened, none had ever closed, and all were profitable.

Then Hong Kong happened. With Hong Kong's reversion from British to Chinese rule set for 1997, Vancouver saw a surge of Hong Kongers relocating there in the 1990s. Given Canada's friendly immigration policy for fellow Commonwealth members, many Hong Kongers used this period to take out Canadian citizenship, purchase property in Vancouver, and enroll in local schools. Then, as the Handover passed without incident, many of these Hong Kongers returned to Hong Kong, but retained both their Canadian citizenship and their Vancouver orientation—including a taste for Tim's homemade fudge.

Partly because of this, Tim opened up a shop at the Vancouver airport. Interestingly, he saw that the sale of fudge and confectionaries accounted for over 90 percent of his business there. Many Hong Kongers and other visitors purchased his prized fudge for gifts when they returned to Hong Kong. Tim experimented with gift boxes and sturdier packaging for the plane journeys, and they were a great success.

Then Tim started getting inquiries: *When are you going to open in Hong Kong? Why not a shop in Hong Kong?* Hong Kong hosted 250,000 Canadian citizens in its population of eight million—by themselves enough to constitute a mid-size town. Indeed, Tim already enjoyed success with his shops in Canadian towns with populations smaller than 250,000.

So why not Hong Kong?

Closing the Capability Gap as a Key Business Issue

In the previous chapter we pointed out that the skills that enable you to win in your home market may not be the same as the ones that you'll need for export market success. Also, some of your skills may not be transportable. We also pointed out that although you should target export markets that place a premium on your most valuable skills, you may still find yourself lacking all the capabilities you need to win in an export market.

Let's make a conceptual point here: in organizational terms, the act of going abroad allows the business to reinvent or redefine itself. In the home market, the business undertakes a cluster of activities, some of which may be core success drivers, others of which may be tasks or functions that have simply accrued over the years. Additionally, in the home market the business has attained a certain scale that allows it to more efficiently manage activities in-house.

In this context, going into a new market entails three steps. First, you must think through what your business's core activities are and which you could do without in a new market. Second, think through how the requirements of the new market might differ. Third, decide whether it makes sense to outsource activities currently undertaken in-house.

All of this must be balanced against that cardinal rule: keep it simple. You will have to weigh the efficiencies and improvements of reengineering the company against the management complexities.

Step one in closing the capabilities gap is for you to improve your own game. How can you improve your knowledge of exporting? Reading this book is a good first step, but you need to build on this experience by learning more about exporting. Look to your local chamber of commerce for seminars and training on exporting. Connect with your government's export promotion agency for their training. State and local governments may offer similar programs. Think about trade missions and trade fairs that would expose you to international commerce. Check with your bank, your law firm, your express delivery firm, and your accounting firm to see whether they have any advice.

Regardless of how you pursue your own export education, you are going to need extra help from the outside. Just because you lack a certain skill doesn't mean you should shy away from that export market. Rather, it suggests that you need to find a way to obtain any missing skills you need to compete in the export market. You could try to build the missing capabilities by hiring people with the skills you need. You could completely outsource the capabilities to a third party that has the expertise. Or you could find partners that can help you close these capability gaps. Many companies need to find partners to help distribute their products and provide local customer service. Others may choose partners who can help them build awareness of their product and its benefits.

Also, let's define "partners" to mean any collaborative relationship. It might be a joint venture or a formal partnership. It might be someone who is hired for service. It might be someone who participates in profits—a licensee or a franchisee. "Partner" is an umbrella term for the many ways that you can bring the needed skills to your business.

Choosing the right partner can boost your company's odds of export market success. Picking the wrong one can be devastating. That's why you'll need to pick your partner in a disciplined fashion. We'll discuss the details later in the chapter; at this point it's worth pointing out that you should get your list of potential partners from people you trust.

Next, you should check whether your prospects have had any business or legal problems. Talk to other companies who have worked with them to find out whether they have happy customers. Obviously you want partners who have a track record of doing a good job for their clients, but there is no substitute for doing your own due diligence to make sure you're working with the right partner.

To that end, here are six issues that you should consider:

1. How can you identify your company's capability gap?
2. How can you determine whether to grow a skill or find it outside the firm?
3. How can you get a good list of potential partners for consideration?
4. What criteria should you use to screen that list of potential partners?
5. How can you conduct effective due diligence on potential partners?
6. How should you structure your relationship with the partner(s) you ultimately select?

Key Research Findings on These Issues

Our research and the case studies that follow suggest that if you can answer "Yes" to the following six questions, you are well on your way to deploying the capabilities that your company needs to succeed in export markets.

1. **Can you identify your company's capability gap?** The answer differs for each company, but if you're following our recommendations throughout this book, it's likely you will, as a minimum, seek partners in marketing and distribution. Some of the cases that follow explore what small business owners have learned from their efforts to that end.

2. **Can you determine whether to grow a skill or find it outside the firm?** You can answer "Yes" to this question if you can make an objective estimate of the costs and benefits of each option and pick the option for which the benefits most exceed the costs. The hard part is quantifying these costs and benefits. In particular, many companies underestimate the cost of motivating a partner, finding out what the partner is doing for your company, and receiving proceeds due in a timely manner. The hidden cost here is the cost of management.

3. **Can you get a good list of potential partners for consideration?** There are many possible sources. If your country has a service that helps SMEs export, chances are good that this service may be able to offer you some names to consider in many countries where you may want to export. (See the list, Selected Export Promotion Agencies, later in this chapter.) If not, see whether your lawyer, accountant, or banker has contacts they trust in those countries that could help you develop a list of candidates. Additionally, look at business and professional associations in your target country.

4. **Can you apply a robust set of criteria to evaluate potential partners?** Our research suggests that you should pick a partner for whom your business is an important priority. This is crucial, because if your product is near the bottom of the list of a partner's priorities, you will not get what you need from the partnership. Another possible risk is that if

a distributor is already handling competitors' products, you could be in for some rough sailing. Such experience would mean the distributor understands your industry—but it could also mean you'd be competing for that distributor's attention. For both of these reasons, plus the likelihood that you simply can't know ahead of time how well you'll work together, it's helpful to test out a partner for between six and twelve months before signing a longer-term agreement.

5. **Can you conduct effective due diligence on potential partners?** You'll need to get access to people who have worked with the distributors in the past and ask them hard questions. Ask current and former customers whether the potential partner delivered value and whether that partner caused any problems. Check with regulators, industry associations, credit rating agencies, and other independent parties to find out about the potential partner's legal, regulatory, and financial track record. You may even want to talk with current and former employees to learn about how the firm treats its people. After all, happy employees are more likely to make customers happy.

6. **Can you structure your relationship with the partner(s) you ultimately select?** Our research suggests that you and your partner should agree up front about your goals for the partnership. This may seem obvious, but it's surprising how many partners—on both sides—fail to do this. Then you should pick a means of getting paid that helps each of you achieve those goals. Ideally, you and your partner should share not only the beneficial returns of the relationship, but also the costs and risks. However, some partnerships are simply contractual relationships. You should also agree on explicit terms for the control of bank accounts and the timing of payments. Moreover, you should start off the relationship with a clear understanding of the conditions that would allow either party to end it and the terms of such dissolution. As illustrated in Figure 7.1, such partnerships can range in their level of engagement from a contractual relationship to a true sharing. The simpler the activity, the simpler the relationship. You might want to start with a very simple arrangement—delivery and warehouse services offered on a per-item basis. If that works

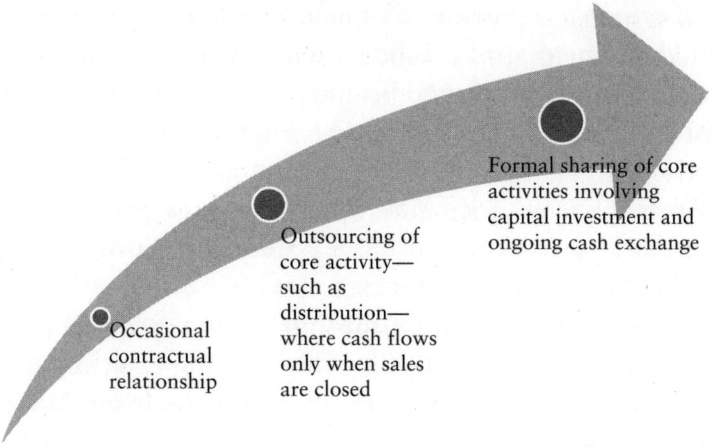

Formal sharing of core
activities involving
capital investment and
ongoing cash exchange

Outsourcing of
core activity—
such as
distribution—
where cash flows
only when sales
are closed

Occasional
contractual
relationship

FIGURE 7.1   Spectrum of Partnership Arrangements

out, you can add customer relationship activities, returns, and repairs. The point is to start simple and allow the relationship to grow—again, with mutual discussion and agreement at increments—as it proves itself.

In addition, we recommend moving incrementally with a partnership. Realize that in the early months you will have to provide extra management time and oversight to ensure that activities are being carried out in the right way. You will want the flexibility to increase or decrease the roles of the partnership as performance warrants. For example, it might make sense to start a warehouse relationship on a six-month contract, to test a law firm by asking them to draw up papers for incorporation and registration, or to give one market to one firm and another market to another firm. You should test-drive every relationship to limit the risk and boost the learning.

Closing the Capability Gap: Case Studies

We examine the challenge of closing the capability gap by looking at four case studies:

1. **Halifax Fan,** a small fan-making company in the UK, decided to target the Indian market as a way to boost its sales.

After a systematic process of evaluating forty potential partners, it settled on one that has helped it win new business in India.

2. **BrewDog**, a Scottish brewer, expanded into seventeen countries through distributors whose interest it piqued through effective guerrilla marketing.

3. **Antler**, a United Kingdom-based luggage maker, achieved considerable success in the United States by partnering with a government-run export assistance service.

4. **Sylvan Australia**, a mushroom spawn producer with a dominant position in Australia, built a strong position in Korea by picking the right partner there with help from Australia's Korean embassy.

Halifax Fan

Imagine you run a business that makes an industrial product, and you've operated in your home market for almost fifty years without seeing the need for international expansion. But you set your sights on higher sales, and you realize that you won't be able to get those greater sales as long as the customers you sell to in your home market are shuttering the operations that would need more of your product.

So you look around the world for other markets that are growing. But once you find such a growing market that you think will need your product, how can you get sales there?

For one British company, that export market was India, and the answer was to find a distribution partner there. Halifax Fan Ltd., founded in 1965, designs and manufactures customized industrial fans. Based in Britain's Yorkshire, Halifax Fan employs a staff of fifty-three. According to Halifax Fan's managing director Malcolm Staff, a joint venture with an Indian manufacturer enabled the company to export to Asia.[1]

To open up that export opportunity, Staff assessed the risks and benefits, researched the markets, and chose the right partner. In 2008, Halifax Fan had identified growth opportunities in Asia but concluded its costs were too high and it could not afford an Asian factory. To find a cost-effective way to tap Asian growth, Halifax Fan decided to form a joint venture with a manufacturer who could build what his UK technical staff designed. Halifax Fan narrowed its search to manufacturers who offered a sales force that could establish an immediate local market presence for Halifax Fan's products.

Halifax Fan was concerned about how it would retain control and protect its investment—and it got help from the UK government. Initially, Halifax Fan researched the Indian market because of the growth opportunities there and its English-speaking population. After conducting research online, Halifax Fan identified forty potential partners, of which it actually visited six.

Staff was underwhelmed by what he saw during his initial visits. For example, a factory he visited early in the process looked to him like a barn. However, he was quite impressed with the quality of its product workmanship. Staff met all six potential partners during his initial visit and made Halifax Fan's final selection during a second visit.

Halifax Fan made that decision by ranking the prospects based on many factors, including their price, financial history, and quality control procedures and results. Once Halifax Fan had selected the winning firm, it brought key Indian employees to the United Kingdom to see the company's operation and to build trust and mutual understanding. Thanks to this partnership, Halifax Fan has won export contracts over competitors who lack a local Indian presence.

(Continued)

Halifax Fan (*Continued*)

Staff learned some lessons along the way. He wishes he had spoken with other businesses that had already gone through the partnering process. He could have accomplished this through the UK government's online resource for business, Business Link or his local chamber of commerce. He also waited too long to hire a local lawyer: "It would have saved time and hassle at the agreement stage if we'd sourced a local lawyer during our trade visits. We left it until we were entering final negotiations, which wasn't ideal."

What lessons should you take from the Halifax Fan case? Here are three:

1. **Decide which capabilities you'll handle in-house and which you'll need to find partners to handle.** Staff developed a clear idea of which capabilities he'd keep—product design—and which he'd need to outsource to an Indian partner—manufacturing and sales. He also did a good job of identifying the criteria that he would use to choose a partner that could best perform these activities for Halifax Fan.

2. **Tap into the experience of other local companies that have exported to the target country.** Staff decided to go it alone when it came to selecting his Indian partners. Although his process started with a long list and visiting the top six was prudent, he might have zeroed in on a list of more likely potential partners and saved himself some time if he had spoken with other companies and experts on the process of seeking external partners.

3. **Work with local experts in the export market from the beginning.** Halifax Fan also decided to wait until the last minute before hiring an attorney local to the potential partner. It would have saved Staff time and might have led to better terms with his chosen partner if he'd had the services of a local legal adviser from the beginning of his partner search process.

BrewDog

Let's say you make a consumer product that gains some notoriety in your home market. But that product is one of hundreds that dot the competitive landscape. Should you then decide to seek growth in an equally crowded export market? If you're going to give that a go, you realize that you may not want to change your business model much.

But you can't expect to succeed in that export market unless you find partners there who can replicate some of the key capabilities that enabled you to make your mark in the home market. If you're up for the challenge of creating the new capabilities through a partnership and adapting them to the export market, this approach can work well.

This is what BrewDog, a Scotland-based artisan brewer founded in 2007 for the UK pub market, needed to do when it decided to export beer to the United States.[2] A key aspect of BrewDog's strategy for the venture was a guerrilla marketing campaign. In July 2010, BrewDog cofounders James Watt and Martin Dickie filmed a four-minute TV pilot for a series on an American network in which they'd evangelize for beer produced by U.S. independent brewers.

In the pilot, they met with quirky artisan beer producers—and the meetings were interspersed with clips of them smashing bottles of "famous lager brands with golf clubs, shooting one with a shotgun, clay pigeon style, and flattening the rest with a bowling ball." Why do Watt and Dickie express their violence toward these big established brands? Watt said, "We've got the same attitude to the incumbents of the beer market as the punks had to pop culture. We're rebelling against bland, corporate, industrially produced beer."

(*Continued*)

BrewDog (*Continued*)

Although if the full tv series was produced they would need to take a series of four-week breaks from BrewDog, the cofounders say the benefits "in terms of getting your name out there in the industry" would definitely outweigh the costs.

When the company was still nascent, Watt and Dickie sent a sample of their home brew to well-known beer and whisky writer Michael Jackson. He urged them to "quit their jobs and establish a brewery," and the pair paid heed. They pooled their US$78,000 of savings, US$47,000 from the bank, and a small loan from the Prince's Scottish Youth Business Trust. With it, they bought some second-hand brewing equipment and set it up in their home town of Fraserburgh, a coastal fishing town north of Aberdeen in Scotland.

Their decision to export came early in their development, because local customers were not buying their product—preferring a cheaper and more pedestrian beer—and the company was quickly using up its scarce capital. The fear of going out of business sent the cofounders outside Scotland, to Scandinavia and North America, in search of true beer aficionados.

Lacking cash and traditional marketing expertise, they decided to combine the guerrilla marketing that had led to their founding with a search for distribution partners. Before approaching potential partners, they identified the most influential beer writers in each market and sent them samples. "We got fantastic reviews and coverage. When we went to the distributors, we said, 'We've done the marketing for you, all you've got to do is sell it.'" BrewDog partnered with distinct distributors in each territory. By July 2010 their products were available in seventeen countries, and international sales accounted for 65 percent of revenues.

They also take an innovative approach to financing their business. In 2009, BrewDog was at the stage where it needed to raise capital to finance its growth. However, given the weak conditions in the financial markets, banks turned down the company's requests for loans. So BrewDog set up a web site where people who drank its beer could buy shares in the company at a minimum investment of US$374. It ultimately raised US$1.2 million from 1,500 investors—after making the investment required to comply with British financial regulations, including a full audit on its accounts.[3]

By the end of 2010, BrewDog had achieved even greater popularity. It was selling its product in twenty-seven countries—earning 85 percent of its revenues outside of Scotland and 70 percent outside of the United Kingdom. Moreover, the company generated US$6.5 million in revenues and US$601,000 in net income.[4]

BrewDog's experience inspired James Watt, its "Head of Stuff," to offer some lessons to exporters. Here are three:

1. **Pick the right partners.** When BrewDog first began to export to Sweden, there were four or five major distributors on its initial list. It then talked with other beer companies and got background information on each of the potential partners. Based on that, BrewDog developed a short list of two or three and met with each in person, listening to their pitch on how they could develop the market for its product in Sweden. BrewDog picked the partner that was not so big that its products would get lost in the mix, but big enough so it had the resources to support the product and would benefit meaningfully from its success.

2. **Manage cash flows carefully.** BrewDog pays for its raw materials—such as hops, malt, and bottles—when

(*Continued*)

BrewDog (*Continued*)

they are ordered, but it typical industry practice is for distributors to pay after sixty days. To speed up its payments, BrewDog offers a 3-percent discount if cash is received in ten days. But these partners are in the minority—must pay before BrewDog ships its product to them. Only rock-solid partners—such as those in Sweden and Norway, which are government-owned—do not have to pay before BrewDog delivers.

3. **Market by turning your weakness into a competitive advantage.** When BrewDog got started, it could not afford the cost of TV advertising, billboards, and print advertisements that the typical large brewer uses to market its product. BrewDog found that social media— including social networks, bloggers, and videos—were both affordable and effective ways to reach its audience. Watt noted that a one-page magazine advertisement in the UK might reach a few potential customers for US$8,000; however, BrewDog was able to reach 250,000 people around the world with a humorous YouTube-style video that it created for US$2,400.[5]

We would add two more lessons:

1. **Distribution partnerships can help establish such export beachheads while limiting risk.** To reach these customers, it's critical to form distribution partnerships— particularly those that do not involve up-front cash investments. If partners are properly motivated, these low-risk deals can help you to find sufficient customers in the export markets.

2. **When seeking export distribution partners, make them enthusiastic about your product before striking a deal.** BrewDog offers an excellent lesson in how to get

distributors interested in your product before you approach them. Those distributors are most likely to be loyal to the products that give them the most profit and will be reluctant to add a new product unless it is clear that it will make them better off. BrewDog got influential columnists on its side in those export markets before approaching distributors there. That made all the difference in its ability to get its product into twenty-seven countries.

Antler

Imagine that you have developed a popular product in your home country and you've been doing a great job of generating steady sales for decades from your fellow citizens. Then along comes a painful economic slowdown that hits your home country hard. You decide that it's time to diversify your customer base. And you hope you can achieve that growth in export markets without spending too much of your dwindling cash reserves.

One way to achieve that is to seek help from a government agency that helps you get access to global distributors and provides some financial assistance to keep you from risking your cash on such international expansion.

That's what a British luxury luggage company called Antler did to gain access to the U.S. market. Antler has been successful in Britain since the 1920s but has made a real effort to export only recently. When it opened a new office in Chicago in 2010, it was Antler's biggest move since relocating from England's Midlands to Bury, in the Greater Manchester area, in 1962. And it achieved significant success with that move to the

(*Continued*)

Antler (*Continued*)

United States—exceeding expectations and gaining customers all over the country.[6]

Antler's U.S. export success was helped by the British government. Antler Sales Manager Claire Willoughby, determined to devise an active strategy for expanding their international trade, contacted UK Trade & Investment (UKTI). According to Willoughby, "Antler has always had some export business but the approach was reactive rather than proactive. We had a very British attitude, and just dealt with orders as they came in rather than making a concerted effort to trade overseas, so I made contact with UK Trade & Investment to make the most of our overseas potential."

UKTI offered a service that helped Antler find the right partners in the United States. To tap into that service, Willoughby and her International Trade Adviser Karen Holden asked UKTI's Overseas Market Introduction Service (OMIS)—which connects businesses with UKTI staff overseas in over a hundred embassies and consulates—to produce a report to identify the best opportunities and find partners. These staff helped Antler gather the best country- and sector-specific information and introduced the company to buyers and distributors.

For Antler, the OMIS identified a contact in the UK consulate in New York who helped kick off its U.S. export strategy. The consulate's Lauren Stone provided an OMIS report, and Willoughby travelled to San Diego, California, in March 2008 to exhibit at the Travel Goods show. Stone's team paved the way with mailings announcing Antler's arrival and contacted key buyers with announcements and literature before the show.

The market response was enthusiastic. According to Willoughby, "People literally wanted to buy our samples off the stand. We had great feedback, and thanks to the OMIS report we had lots of contacts. I spent time after the show visiting America, speaking to retailers and looking at prices and positioning, and we employed a sales manager for the United States, Andrew Hamilton, who flew out in October to set up our office in Chicago and look at suppliers."

By 2010, Antler had 7,500 square feet of warehousing space in Chicago and five agents in the United States. Antler also began to recruit American staff. In March 2010, Antler sent the first stock and quickly won over twenty customers. Willoughby said, "Although the brand was unknown in America, it is selling well already—we spent a lot of time researching prices and positioning, and we are thrilled with the sales figures so far."

Her approach to selecting distributors was to find independent dealers who would support the upscale positioning of the brand. According to Willoughby, "We are distributing through respected, independent retailers who can help build the brand rather than large chains who would insist on huge discounts. We intend to stay in the market for the long term, and to sell our ranges on their features and benefits. . . . Over 70 percent of initial customers have already reordered, and we are confident that the Antler brands will become as well known and well respected in the USA as they are in the UK."

Ultimately, Antler's partnership with the UK's OMIS service has yielded a significant payoff, as it attempts to grow beyond its dominant position in the UK market. As a result of its initial success using OMIS to generate U.S. sales, Antler is tapping the service to expand into other countries. Not long after commissioning a new OMIS report for Canada, Antler began trading there and is already receiving repeat orders.

(*Continued*)

Antler (*Continued*)

Antler has gone on to commission OMIS reports for Spain and Japan, and by mid-2010 was generating 10 percent of sales outside the United Kingdom, with a goal of continuing to increase that share.

Antler's dominant market position in the United Kingdom made exporting a logical and vital next step. In the UKTI and OMIS service, the company found the partners it needed to get established overseas and achieve early success.

What lessons about closing the capability gap can you take from this case? Here are two:

1. **Work with export experts to plot your strategy.** If your country offers a service like UKTI, take advantage of its resources. Antler clearly got significant value from the price it paid for the reports that helped it find distributors in export markets—so much value that Antler decided to use it again as it sought to expand beyond its initial export market. Much of the insight from such agencies is available to people from all nations, such as country studies. However, direct support and consultations are usually limited to businesses from the relevant country. (See the list of major agencies later in this chapter.)

2. **Pick distributors that buy into your brand positioning.** The OMIS reports were a huge help to Antler, but the service would not have been so helpful if OMIS had ended up picking a distributor that would try to cheapen its brand by cutting prices to penetrate the biggest retailers. Instead, Antler wisely chose to focus on distributors who would preserve its upscale brand positioning.

Sylvan Australia

Let's say you produce an agricultural product in your home country that manufacturers use to make their products. Your product is well accepted in your home market, but you find that growth at home is limited. So you decide to target an export market in Asia. You find that the Asian market has different uses for your product, and the customers who buy it are in different industries than those in your home market. Do you seek a partner or decide that the Asian market is too different from your home market, so you punt?

That was the choice facing Sylvan Australia Pty Ltd, a producer of so-called spawn, the equivalent of mushroom seed. Sylvan Australia is a subsidiary of an American fungal technology company, Sylvan Inc. The company also offers supplementary products and services for mushroom growers. Sylvan decided that it could partner with a company in Korea to tap the growth opportunity there. The process of forming Sylvan's Korean joint venture was led by Marion Lawson, general manager of Sylvan Australia.[7]

Although Sylvan had achieved success, Lawson was concerned about slowing growth. Its business and mushroom markets were maturing, and Lawson believed that Sylvan's best path to maintaining its growth was to develop new products that tapped Sylvan's core competencies. Sylvan scanned the competitive environment for new growth industries and new markets. It also fought to maintain its 70-percent Australian market share by providing excellent customer service and out-innovating its competitors.

Sylvan based its choice of Korean partners on their ability to sell to both business and government customers.

(*Continued*)

Sylvan Australia (*Continued*)

Thus Lawson gained confidence in the prospects for Sylvan's long-term growth in Korea and its operation there as a basis for expansion into other Asian countries. Moreover, Sylvan was able to establish a first in its industry—becoming the first foreign company to be granted a permit to import mushroom seed under Korean Seed Law. Lawson hoped that its presence in Korea would scale up to the point that it would construct a production facility there with its Korean partners.

Lawson offered practical advice for companies seeking to export: "work from the market back." To that end, she suggested that exporting companies take these steps:

- Assure themselves that the export market will be willing to pay for their product due to the value it creates for export market customers.
- Make sure their distributors understand their product and can provide technical support for it.
- Understand the supply chain in the countries where they're exporting.
- Gain insight into the business and cultural differences.
- Use the services of a government export service such as Austrade (see the list of selected export promotion agencies that follows). (In Sylvan's case, Austrade's Seoul office "was instrumental in securing business in Korea. It has been a good partnership, and continues to be so.")
- Communicate clearly the terms of trade with export partners—ensuring that all agreements and understandings are well documented.
- Learn the tax and legal implications relating to trade between the home country and the exporting country.
- Comply with all regulatory rules and laws in the export country.

Selected Export Promotion Agencies

- U.S. Department of Commerce (www.commerce.gov)
- Japan External Trade Organization (www.jetro.go.jp)
- Australia's Austrade (www.austrade.gov.au/)
- UK Trade & Investment (UKTI) (www.ukti.gov.uk)
- Canada's Export Development Canada (www.edc.ca/)
- Singapore's Ministry of Trade and Industry (www.app.mti.gov.sg/)

Closing the Capability Gap to Take Overseas Market Share

Let's recap what executives can do to close the capability gap and win in export markets. Here's a six-step methodology to use:

1. **Identify the capabilities that your company lacks for winning in the export market.** At the end of Chapter Six, you should have identified these capabilities. For example, to pick partners to provide distribution or manufacturing, you must clearly identify the capabilities for which you'll seek partners.
2. **Develop the criteria for picking partner candidates.** Using these criteria, rank the partner candidates and select the winner. The criteria might include the price they charge for their services, their reputation for quality, how much attention they will be able to devote to your product or service, and the strength of their network among customers and regulators in the export market.
3. **Talk to experts who have contacts and exporting know-how in your selected export market.** From their ranks, assemble a team of experts who can help you find a list of partner candidates that are likely to score well on your criteria. These experts might include lawyers, regulatory experts, CEOs of companies that have exported successfully to the country in

question, and government export advisors. These experts may suggest refinements to your partner selection criteria, and they should offer you names of potential partners.

4. **Develop a list of partner candidates and short-list them by applying the selection criteria.** Conduct due diligence on the partner candidates in areas related to each of your selection criteria. Once you've developed insight into how well the partner candidates meet your criteria, you can rank the candidates and pick the top five or six for more in-depth research.

5. **Visit each partner candidate on the short list.** While visiting, try to assess your level of comfort with the partner candidates' top executives, their customers' level of satisfaction, and the depth of their network within the export country.

6. **Select the winning partner and structure a mutually beneficial contract.** In this final step, revise your assessment of each of the short-listed candidates based on each of the criteria, and pick the partner that best satisfies them. Once you've selected the winner, structure an agreement with the partner that will create incentives for both parties to work hard to achieve their shared goals—and make it clear how each side can gracefully exit the partnership if those goals are not being achieved.

Key Lessons from Tim's Homemade Fudge

Tim has a number of strengths and also some severe limitations. His strengths are that he is a solid, successful businessman with a product and a model that are respected in the market. His main limitation is that he has a small and insular management team (largely his own family members) with limited experience outside the core activities of the firm. His small team also inhibits his ability to expand.

Tim really has two businesses: his fudge/confectionary business and his lunch counter/sandwich business. In his home market of Canada these two businesses fit together nicely; in the United States this seems to work too.

But his experience at the Vancouver airport shows that the international clientele values his candy much more than his sandwiches. He has built a respected brand, and he is selling a welcome gift item.

Tim should indeed explore expansion in Hong Kong, but he should be aware of his weaknesses in this regard. His core weakness is that he has no ability to manage a facility from such a distance. His second weakness is that because this customer base is much more interested in his candies, he is unlikely to succeed there with the same product mix.

Tim decided to sell his fudge in Hong Kong through a leading department store. He did some direct research and also worked with the Hong Kong Economic and Trade Directorate. The Export Development Canada helped identify leading retail merchants. The British Columbia government had an annual trade mission to Hong Kong, and Tim was able to participate. This allowed him to meet directly with leading Hong Kong merchants and to sign a contract.

A happy ending? You bet. Tim's sales to Hong Kong now exceed his sales in any city outside Vancouver.

Closing the Capabilities Gap Checklist

Have you really closed the capability gap so you can take a meaningful share of export markets? To answer that question positively, you should have already developed detailed answers to the following questions.

Questions

If you were starting your company all over from scratch, which activity might you contract out, such as manufacturing, distribution, and so on? Which activity is absolutely central to your business success?

What is the simplest way for your firm to enter a new market? Can you start by simply exporting to customers, or do you need a more complicated structure?

Can you close your capability gap simply by working with local counterparts to your domestic support—such as bankers, lawyers, and accountants—or do you need to partner with other locals?

Conclusion

If you want to win export market share, you'll need to be able to compete on several dimensions in the export market. Most likely, these will include distributing your product or service. And in order to get your products to customers in that export market, you'll need to follow a disciplined approach to finding the best partner and forging a relationship with that partner that aligns your interests with those of your partner. Following the advice in this chapter will boost your odds of success.

Notes

1. Details of the Halifax Fan case and quotes are drawn from "Halifax Fan," Businesslink.gov.uk, accessed September 15, 2010, http://www.businesslink.gov.uk/bdotg/action/detail?itemId=1076888388&type=CASE+STUDIES.
2. BrewDog case details and quotes are drawn from Peter Cohan's January 2011 interview with BrewDog head James Watt, and from James Hurley, "Export Focused Craft Brewer Seek Route Into UK Pub Market," *Telegraph UK*, July 15, 2010, http://www.telegraph.co.uk/finance/businessclub/7891975/Export-focused-craft-brewer-seeks-route-into-UK-pub-market.html.
3. Peter Cohan's interview with James Watt, January 5, 2011.
4. Ibid.
5. Ibid.
6. Details of the Antler case are drawn from "Antler," Greater Manchester Chamber of Commerce web site, accessed September 15, 2010, http://www.gmchamber.co.uk/go-global/ go-global/casestudies.
7. Details of the Sylvan Australia case are drawn from "Sylvan Australia," Austrade web site, accessed September 15, 2010, http://www.austrade.gov.au/Case-studies-from-Women-in-Export/default.aspx.

PART THREE

WHEN: MAKING YOUR EXPORT STRATEGY HAPPEN

Chapter Eight

RESOURCE THE STRATEGY

"Whose idea was this, anyway?" Pedro Tomasina asked of no one in particular. "We were doing just fine before we started selling to the United States."

Pedro is CEO of Kitchen Corp., a small firm in Monterrey, Mexico, that makes specialty kitchenware for restaurants. His outburst was half-joking, but his exasperation was real. The joke was that everyone knew full well that the decision to enter the U.S. market had been made by Pedro personally. Although the kitchen utensils he manufactured and sold were not a particularly high-tech product, Pedro took pride in their durability and utility. "Serious tools for serious cooks" was his slogan—and Pedro had earned a strong reputation for excellent equipment. Word of mouth was an important tool for Pedro, which was fortunate, because Pedro had a small management and sales team. A typical entrepreneur with a passion for his product, Pedro was a tireless manager as well as an accomplished amateur cook himself. Indeed, he often found that he could close and keep major accounts by demonstrating his skills in the kitchen. Pedro manufactured in Monterrey and sold through his own showrooms and catalog sales across Mexico. After just ten years of production, Pedro's sales already topped US$40 million.

Pedro had noticed two recent trends in his business. First, for the past three years the company's growth had been over 10 percent per year, and it looked like that trend was set to continue as Pedro plowed operating profits back into the company—building out his sales team to ten full-time sales people and constantly refreshing and expanding his product line.

Second, Pedro had started to get international orders. Most of these came from the United States, but he also received e-mail orders from across the Western Hemisphere and even a few from other countries. All of this took place without any international marketing or advertising. In fact, his catalog was printed only in Spanish, and all items were priced in Mexican pesos.

Pedro was intrigued. If he could potentially sell several hundred thousand dollars in the United States with no effort, why not put a plan into place?

Pedro's management was ambivalent, but Pedro discounted that believing that it was due to the fact that no one on his team had any particular U.S. experience. People tend to fear what they do not understand, he reasoned.

So Pedro reached out. He hired a bright young bilingual salesman who could work in the United States. He targeted the border towns of southern and central Texas to start. He printed the catalog in American English and opened a U.S. bank account to take payment in U.S. dollars.

A year later, what were the results? Pedro's sales were up to almost US$43 million: a nice number, but representing 8 percent growth—his lowest growth rate in over five years. Worse, the U.S. sales came in at only a few hundred thousand dollars. Pedro still received some over-the-transom orders from the United States, so total U.S. sales were up a bit, but far below expectations.

What had gone wrong? More important, what should Pedro do now?

Resource the Strategy as a Key Business Issue

In the previous five chapters, we examined how you can formulate a successful export strategy. But the work does not stop there. After all, if you have an export strategy but you don't act on it, you might as well not even have bothered to create it in the first place. As we'll describe in the remainder of this book, implementing your export strategy depends on investing in needed resources, hurdling cultural barriers, and taking concrete action.

In this chapter, we focus on the first of these three strategic elements—the resources. What resources will you need? Most likely, implementing your export strategy will require capital and talent. Of course, the required capital depends on the specifics of your export strategy. If that strategy depends on building a warehouse, hiring workers, and renting a fleet of trucks, then you'll need some form of capital to pay for all that. And you may want to hire someone to watch over those resources.

But as we've advised throughout this book, it may be better for you to start small. If you take that advice, then you may need enough capital to ship your product to your distribution partner, but from there your partner will take over the cost. And such a partnership probably does not require you to hire a full-time person to manage it. Instead, you could assign a manager to spend a day or two a month visiting the distributor and checking in every day via e-mail or telephone to keep closer tabs on how things are progressing with the export strategy.

Starting small means conducting a frugal experiment and then learning from its outcome. If the experiment leads to an export profit, then you may want to explore ways to dedicate more resources to make more export profits.

If the experiment is a money loser, then you'll want to examine the reasons for the failure and whether it's possible to do things differently to boost results. It's possible you will conclude that the export strategy is so flawed that it's time to pull the plug on it and perhaps reconsider the entire thing.

Another key point about resourcing your export strategy is that this is the time when you find out how serious you are about the venture. If you have been thinking that an export strategy would be a nice add-on, a hard-nosed consideration of the resources required to implement that strategy will test how much you are willing to invest in it.

Remember, a business in a new market is in some respects a start-up business. And many start-ups require disproportionate time and money. It is not usual for a thirty-person business to have US$10 million in sales in the home market. However, this same business may well discover that it requires the equivalent of a half-time person to manage market entry in the new market, and that new market generates only US$50,000 in sales in the first year—less than one-sixth the productivity of the home market.

Here are four issues that you should consider:

- How much capital and management time will the strategy require?
- What are the possible sources of those resources?
- How should you decide among the potential candidates?
- How do you formalize this capital and management decision?

Key Research Findings on These Issues

Our research and the case studies that follow suggest that if you can comprehensively answer the preceding four questions, you are well on your way to resourcing the strategy that your company needs to succeed in export markets.

1. How much capital and management time will the strategy require? Theoretically, it should not be too hard to figure out the cost of the resources you'll need to put your export strategy into practice. You need to do research into the actual amount of capital you'll need to perform the key activities you need to get your product into the export market. The key to doing this right is to put together a team with specific expertise in conducting this research. And this means not leaving out any details, while leaving room for unexpected things happening—as they surely will. We advise modest and incremental allocation of resources, but be careful of trying to do things "on the cheap." There will be a threshold of activity an export strategy requires, and you do not want your outlay to fall below that threshold.

2. What are the possible sources of those resources? For management time, you may want to carve out a portion of a trusted manager's schedule to oversee your company's export partnership. But if the export strategy involves a more significant investment, you may need to hire a full-time person to manage the business in that market. Such a person ought to have experience straddling both the home and export markets while building up sales profitably. Meanwhile, you'll need capital to fuel the export strategy; that could come from many places, including current operations, a bank loan, an equity infusion, or a government loan or guarantee.

3. How should you decide among the potential candidates? Your selection criteria will depend on the resource. If you need to hire a manager, you should pick the person based on a track record of achieving growth in similar business situations, demonstrated ability to achieve these results working across cultures, and willingness to work with your firm on terms that will reward your mutual success in the venture. As for capital sources, pick a supplier that can work with you as a longer-term partner and is willing to negotiate deal terms that will help you succeed.

4. How do you formalize this capital and management decision? Given that many export and new market strategies can be a drain on resources, it is important for you to shape internal consensus at your firm. If the company has to allocate US$50,000 extra in travel expenses, this may well be a wise decision, but it suggests that this export program must have an approved budget and that the management of the firm understand that it will require an outlay of resources before there is much to show for it.

Resource the Strategy: Case Studies

We examine the challenge of closing the capability gap by looking at three case studies:

• **GP Graders,** an Australian maker of agricultural equipment, used its country's export finance organization to help it boost export sales dramatically in less than a decade.

- **Robert Mondavi,** a U.S.–based wine maker, partnered with companies in France and Chile so they could share vineyards, winemaking operations, and product development talent to create new wines that captured significant global market share.

- **Footcare International,** an Australia-based maker of shoe insoles, tapped the Australian government's working capital guarantee to finance its international expansion.

GP Graders

If you make a popular piece of equipment and want to export it from your home country, you face a challenge. It's not easy to find a financial institution willing to take the risk of fronting you enough money to ship that product into the export country and wait for repayment until you've successfully sold the product and collected the cash.

That's the problem that GP Graders—a Melbourne, Australia-based manufacturer of fruit-grading and packing machinery—faced when it tried to export its product to Turkey. Fortunately, GP Graders was able to tap the Australian government for a guarantee that would enable it to finance its exports there.[1]

GP Graders was established in 1963 in response to a need for automation in the post-harvest handling of fruit, according to its CEO Stuart Payne. The grading and sorting of fruit was embraced by the fruit industry as a requirement first put forward by buyers and ultimately by consumers, and as a way of achieving a higher average market price for produce.

GP Graders manufactures packing house machinery for the fruit and shellfish industries. It designs and manufactures grading and packing lines to sort produce according to weight, size, color, and separates defective or unacceptable product using camera systems. The company believes that it is a world leader in the cherry industry and is seeking to enter the oyster, abalone, and scallop markets.

GP Graders employs about sixty employees, which varies according to production schedules through the year. It has 500 to 600 active customers, with 700 installations in Australia and 150 installations outside Australia. In 2009 and 2010, 65 percent of the company's revenue came from export sales.

GP Graders first decided to pursue an export market in 2001, after some initial successes in Italy and Norway. GP Graders realized it manufactured a unique product for an expanding niche market and had the experience to sell this product overseas. It believed that its product for the Australian market was superior to competing products being sold outside Australia—making it easier for GP Graders to gain export market share.

Ironically, the country GP Graders most actively targeted initially was the country in which it had the least success—the United States. It seems that many companies first gain traction in the U.S. market and expand from there, whereas GP Graders had great success in Turkey, Chile, Italy, and Greece. GP Graders' export market success was based on demand pull rather than supply push. Payne said, "It was not so much that we chose those countries; it was that those countries chose us. Our success stemmed from putting a huge effort into our first installations in each of those countries and making the first site the reference site for all other sales. Sales then expanded within that country and into other countries as our reputation developed. Success certainly did not happen without devoted effort."

The countries in which GP Graders had the most success were those that had undergone the greatest

(*Continued*)

GP Graders (*Continued*)

expansion in the industries that require its products and those with the most compelling reasons to reduce their manual input. High-labor-cost countries are compelled to use technology because it automates the produce packing process. Countries that have expanded plantings of crop varieties that GP Graders handles on its machinery purchase its products to meet the increased volume of supply. GP Graders was also confident it would win business in those countries, as it had a competitively superior product and know-how.

GP Graders tries to customize its product to each market as much as possible without losing manufacturing efficiencies. Payne explained, "We worked very closely with customers to develop a product that had a generic application and were careful not to take a generic product and customize it too finely, as we would lose manufacturing scale. We have refined our product range and designs to cater to all commercial-sized customers. Our designs include the best-quality third-party parts available to avoid warranty claims, as the cost [of] overseas warranty is magnified several-fold compared to domestic market claims. Also central to strategy was branding. The GP Graders brand is front and center on everything we sell."

GP Graders have exported machinery to sixteen countries (among them are Slovakia, Norway, Syria, and Iran). It supplies nine of the top ten cherry packers in Chile, the top ten cherry packers in Turkey, the top five in Greece, three of the top five in Italy, and the top ten in Australia. By 2010, GP Graders was targeting all major seafood suppliers in Australia before taking that expertise overseas.

When negotiating to sell equipment to a buyer in Turkey, GP Graders got help from Australia's Export Finance and Insurance Corporation (EFIC) to help structure a competitive finance package. Under the deal, GP Graders received payments for the equipment by means of a letter of credit for US$491,100, issued by a Turkish bank. EFIC provided a letter of credit to Westpac, GP Graders' bank, which guaranteed the payments due from the Turkish bank under the letter of credit.

By this arrangement the buyer paid the Turkish bank for the equipment over a five-year period, whereas GP Graders received payment after it presented specific documents to Westpac verifying that it had provided the equipment.

EFIC's service proved critical to GP Graders' market expansion. According to Payne, EFIC's involvement in the Turkish deal made possible the buyer's five-year payment term, which proved to be a "deal winner. With the cost of machines in the vicinity of US$1 million, it's important to be able to put together financing packages that help us gain a competitive advantage in these major deals."

GP Graders appeared to have benefited tremendously from this financing arrangement. According to Payne, "In 2001, only 5 percent of our business was export. . . . [By 2010 it was] 75 percent, to countries such as Turkey, Greece, Chile, and Italy."

GP Graders has learned some important lessons from its exporting experience. Payne pointed out, "We have changed our agency agreements to place more responsibility on our agency network through the sales process, design stages, closing of sales and warranty issues that may arise. This has come about through knowledge gained from experience and by GP Graders being a lot more selective about agents and their expectations. Bad agents can do great damage to your brand in new markets, from which it can be very difficult to recover."

In general, GP Graders has enjoyed success with its export strategy. According to Payne, "Our timing to enter

(*Continued*)

GP Graders (*Continued*)

markets has been right, the agents we have chosen in our key markets have been right, the product range we have offered has been right, and our honest approach to customers has been right. We have not fallen into the trap of increasing the customers' expectations beyond what we are capable of delivering, which means we always have satisfied customers."

Payne offers some important lessons for exporters: "The world is a big place, and once you are out there opportunities can arise from the strangest of places. We are quoting on projects in Romania and Uzbekistan at present. Other lessons would be managing currency and having a firm strategy in place and always, always, always insist on letters of credit from a rated bank."

He also had some useful suggestions for first-time exporters. Payne said, "Try to use agency relationship before any direct investments in markets are made, as it minimizes potential losses if the market doesn't work out the way you would like. There are no setup costs beyond training and marketing. Make sure *you* 'own' the customer, not the agent, as the customer relationship should always continue, where the agency relationship may not."

GP Graders also offered some practical ideas about how best to manage currency risk. Payne advises, "Try to quote in your domestic currency and convert into another currency only on signing of a contract. Currency volatility on a high-value sale can be extremely costly or extremely profitable, but if currency speculation is not your core business, then without a hedging program or strategy to manage this you might be gambling with the success of your business."

What lessons should you take from the GP Graders case regarding financing your export strategy? Here are two:

1. **Trade finance can help you gain export market share.** In most cases finance is behind the scenes, supporting your firm's export strategy. But it can be a way for your firm to gain market share, because for some products, the price and the terms of payment are critical factors that determine the winning supplier. If you can offer potential customers better value than competitors can, you can use trade finance as a way to gain market share while limiting the financial risk of your export strategy.

2. **Government can help supply trade finance.** In some countries, there are government agencies whose mission it is to help you get that capital. Those agencies may or may not supply the money, but they may partner with capital providers and use their perceived stability as a way to help you get the capital you need. If you're seeking help to finance exports, you should try to find out whether your government can play this role.

Selected Export Finance Agencies

- **United States: Export Import Bank.** Provides working capital guarantees (pre-export financing), export credit insurance, and loan guarantees and direct loans (buyer financing). Eighty-five percent of transactions directly benefit U.S. small businesses.

- **Canada: Export Development Canada.** Provides insurance and financial services and bonding products to 8,300 Canadian companies in 200 markets worldwide.

Eighty percent of EDC's customers are small and medium-sized businesses.

- **Japan: Export Import Bank of Japan.** Provides financing to assist with Japanese corporate export projects.
- **German: Hermes Agency.** Provides US$25 billion worth of guarantees for German exporters—90 percent of which go to Central and Eastern Europe.
- **Australia: Export Finance and Insurance Corporation (EFIC).** EFIC provides loans, contract bonds, and guarantees to support exporters and their exports to forty countries. In fiscal year 2010, it supported exports and overseas investments of A$5.9 billion.

Robert Mondavi

If you've established a successful business in your home market, financing and staffing export initiatives may seem like an unnecessary distraction. You may not want to take your eye off the domestic market ball, especially if the growth at home is slowing down and you need to find a new source of growth to satisfy your investors. But how can you get the resources you need to finance and operate those growing export businesses without taking on too much risk while simultaneously getting the attention and drive needed to make that export strategy pay off?

If you're American wine maker Robert Mondavi Corporation (RMC), you achieve your export goals by sharing resources with partners in different countries. These partnerships involve joint investments, export market advertising and promotion, and shared management of the export market operation.[2]

Specifically, RMC—with 1999 sales of US$370 million— shared and received different resources from its partnerships in France and Chile. By the mid-1990s, RMC had established a partnership in Napa, California, with France's Rothschild family and one in Chile with the Chadwick family. These partnerships resulted in several new global brands, including Opus One and Caliterra.

RMC's first export partnership was unusual because it was really a way for a French winery to enter the U.S. market while helping to boost RMC's brands in the United States. To that end, in 1979 RMC formed a partnership called Opus One with Baron Philippe de Rothschild, owner of Château Mouton-Rothschild in Bordeaux, France.

The partners decide to share materials, know-how, and marketing in a fifty-fifty joint venture. Rothschild initiated the venture because he wanted access to the U.S. market. But Rothschild lacked critical resources to make such a venture work effectively—including knowledge of the local history and people that he believed he needed in order to make a great wine. According to Robert Mondavi, RMC got "over a million dollars' worth of free advertising" when Opus One was announced. That prestige helped the company to form other international partnerships.

Opus One ended up selling very high-priced wines to markets around the world. RMC sold the venture thirty-five acres of its best vineyards and two more vineyards near RMC headquarters, where the Opus One winery was established. After ten years of development, the winery was completed in 1991.

The partners dedicated key people to develop Opus One's first product. Château Mouton-Rothschild's wine-maker, Lucien Sionnea, and RMC's winemaker, Timothy Mondavi, worked together on the first Opus One

(Continued)

Robert Mondavi (*Continued*)

vintage. Over the following five years, the two blended their different cultural styles and winemaking techniques. The partners invested in high-tech facilities, including a barrel room with an electronic climate control system.

The partners ended up creating more demand than they could supply. The result was very high prices. Opus One made just thirty thousand cases per year—each bottle of which sold for between US$90 and US$100 in sixty-five world markets. Distributors and individual customers had to order long before the wine was released. It was America's first ultra-premium wine—and it became quite popular in the French, English, German, and Swiss markets.

RMC's 1996 partnership with Chile's Chadwick family led to the production of wine at a far more modest price. Through this partnership, RMC established a global value chain that produced wine selling for between US$7 and US$10 a bottle. A fifty-fifty joint venture with Chile's Eduardo Chadwick, called Viña Caliterra S.A. produced Caliterra Chilean wines.

The joint venture split up the wine value chain. Chile's Viña Errazuriz Winery produced the wine until the venture's new winemaking facility was built. The Caliterra wine for the U.S. market was shipped in bulk to RMC's Woodbridge facility, where the wine was finished; wine to be sold in the global markets was produced and finished in the Viña Errazuriz Winery. RMC was the sole U.S. distributor of Viña Errazuriz.

Both parties contributed capital to the venture. The goal was to expand the Caliterra operations and to purchase the thousand-hectare La Arboleda Estate in Chile's Colchagua Valley. Viña Caliterra planned to obtain any additional grapes it needed from independent growers in the Colchagua Valley. RMC anticipated that the new

Caliterra Winery would be productive by the 1999 harvest. The Viña Caliterra partnership produced six different wines under the Caliterra label.

And their product was successful in the marketplace. The Caliterra brand was soon one of the fastest-growing import brands. In 1997 Caliterra's global sales reached an estimated three hundred thousand cases.

The RMC case is most relevant for medium-sized firms, but it highlights important lessons for all SMEs. Here are three:

1. **Identify up front the goals and strategy of an export partnership.** Whether you run a small firm looking to export a single product or a larger one seeking to introduce new products into an export market, you won't be able to unlock any resources for your export strategy unless you and your partner share the same goals. As we'll explore later, that partnership also will work only if you share some common values and ways of operating. If you share the same goals and agree on the strategy to achieve them, you'll have a far easier time working with your partner to identify the resources required to put that strategy into practice.

2. **Identify the capital, facilities, management talent, and marketing programs you'll need to launch your export strategy.** As the RMC case illustrates, once partners agree on goals and strategy, they need to consider how best to execute that strategy. In RMC's partnerships, both parties supplied capital, they shared production and distribution resources, they developed new products jointly, and they tapped a common marketing message. Although this level of resource complexity is not going to be required for a small company, the basic message remains—you and your export partner must agree on the additional resources required and find a way to get them.

(Continued)

Robert Mondavi (*Continued*)

3. Be prepared to dedicate people to putting the export strategy into place. RMC and its partners decided to put their best product developers together to create new wine brands in their partnerships in France and Chile. Although a smaller firm might need to dedicate only part of a manager's time to overseeing an export partnership, it is essential for an exporter to work together with a partner to achieve shared goals. To that end, you should put in place the performance measurements and systems needed to track how well that partnership is doing and to make adjustments along the way.

Footcare International

Let's say your business makes a simple consumer product and you want to export it. But if you can generate demand in a new country, you'll have to make enough units to satisfy that demand. Unfortunately, there is a timing challenge here. To make the product for those foreign customers, you'll need to buy the supplies, pay the workers, and operate the machines—but you won't collect the cash from those customers until after you've paid your suppliers and workers to make the product and put it into their hands.

Of course, there are ways around that timing problem. Footcare, an Australian maker of insoles, foot comfort products, and shoelaces, discovered one of them. Working capital guarantees can help exporters get the cash they need to cover them during that cash gap period.

Footcare International is not just any insole maker—it's Australia's largest. But it needed additional working capital to fund more exports to Asia, the United States, the Middle East, India, and Europe.[3] Like GP Graders, Footcare turned to EFIC, but for a different purpose. EFIC assisted Footcare by providing a US$300,000 working capital guarantee to Footcare's bank, ANZ, to help finance its export strategy. EFIC Headway—the name of the guarantee that Footcare used—enables eligible SME exporters to get more working capital from their bank without requiring further security.

By gaining access to the additional working capital, Footcare succeeded in meeting international demand. Barry Kearney, Footcare's managing director, said, "Our sales have been growing strongly in a range of overseas markets, and we needed extra working capital to keep up with international demand for our products. The working capital assistance from EFIC and ANZ is helping us achieve our aim to become the world's number one manufacturer and distributor of insoles and foot comfort products."

What new lessons should you take from the Footcare case? Here are two:

1. **If you have a relationship with a bank, it helps to seek out guarantees for export working capital.** The Footcare case suggests that without an existing banking relationship, it may be difficult to obtain the additional working capital required to finance export production. With such a relationship, you may be able to obtain export working capital if you can get a guarantee. If your government makes such guarantees available, the financing may make the difference between export success and failure.

2. **Pay attention to the timing of export cash flows.** Payment schedules and terms in your new market can differ significantly from your home market conditions. To win in exporting, you will want to try to match the norms of your

(Continued)

Footcare International (*Continued*)

new market, but that may put pressure on your cash flow. You need to project these changes and develop a sense of how you could make up for a drop in cash flow. You could use your own cash reserves or a bank loan, or you could factor in receivables. The point is, if you have not precisely calculated the timing and nature of your export strategy's cash flows, then you could be in for trouble. To meet the requirements of its working capital guarantee, it's likely that Footcare carefully estimated the size of the cash flow gap that would emerge between when it paid suppliers to produce its product and when export market customers would remit their payments to Footcare. This precise calculation likely helped it to obtain the guarantee on its working capital requirements from the government and reassured the bank that extended the financing.

Resourcing the Strategy to Take Overseas Market Share

So what should executives do to assure themselves of the resources their companies will need to execute their export strategy? Here's a four-step methodology to use:

1. **Identify the categories of resources you'll need to execute the export strategy.** Once you've taken the time to forge shared goals and strategy, you ought to identify the broad categories of resources you'll need to get so that you can put that strategy into practice. Most likely, those categories will include capital and management time. But they might also include other resources such as warehouses, trucks, and perhaps even manufacturing facilities.
2. **Estimate how much it will cost to add those resources.** Once you've pulled together a consensus on what resources you'll need in order to put your export strategy into practice, the next step is to figure out how much it will cost to add them.

Try contacting people who have done this in the recent past to find out their actual experience and how much more it cost them than they had originally anticipated. Based on this, you may want to scale back your investment to reflect the real costs.

3. **Calculate the cash flows that this investment is likely to generate.** If you hope to convince capital providers to write you a check to finance your export strategy, you'll need to convince them that their investment will yield an attractive return. To do that, you should develop forecasts of the cash likely to flow from the investment you have estimated at the outset. When you develop these cash flow estimates, make sure to analyze both pessimistic and optimistic scenarios along with your base case.

4. **Get the financing you need from the right capital providers.** Once you've estimated the cash flows associated with your export investment, it's time to find the right providers of the capital needed to help you pay for them. You'll need to network in order to find the right banks or investors for your particular project, and then find a person in the bank who understands your goals and has the clout to get a fast and accurate response to your questions. Whichever capital provider you pick, make sure you understand and are comfortable with their contract terms.

Lessons for Kitchen Corp.

Pedro failed to fully appreciate the opportunity costs of entering the U.S. market. The key was that his domestic sales were growing at a very healthy 10-percent-plus rate, and he needed to be cautious about doing anything that might disrupt that pattern. Along the same lines, he seemed to misread the incidental orders he received from other countries as a sign of strong market interest.

Additionally, no one at Pedro's firm had any particular expertise in the United States, and no one at the firm endorsed the idea or expressed confidence in the initiative. Perhaps Pedro's instincts were right, but he should have taken other views into account.

Another concern was that his domestic sales were spurred by word of mouth. In the United States, Pedro would enjoy no such advantage. If he sold his product through personal cooking appearances, how could that work in the United States? He was going into a new market as an unknown.

Pedro would be well advised to take a step back and make three decisions. First, he should return his home market sales to 10-percent-plus growth by devoting his personal energy exclusively to the home market. Second, he should translate his web site into American English and maintain his U.S. bank account for web orders. Third, he should identify a U.S. distributor who will handle his sales for a commission, thus taking the management burden of exporting off his shoulders.

Resource the Strategy Checklist

Have you really figured out how to get the resources you'll need to put your export strategy into practice? To answer that question positively, you should be able to answer "Yes" to all of the following questions.

Questions	Answers (Yes or No)
Do you have a formal budget and timetable for your export plan?	
Can you make your strategy an incremental one?	
Have you determined the minimum amount of money required to enter the target market, and confirmed its feasibility for your plan?	
Does your management understand the resource commitment the new market requires? Has this been formalized in a presentation, and has a budget been approved?	
Do you know how you will finance your export strategy? Can you afford that from your available cash or lines of credit?	

Conclusion

Once you've developed an export strategy, the true test of your commitment to it is whether you get the additional capital and management time required to make that strategy happen. Companies that have achieved success with their export strategies have been able to get the capital and management talent they needed to gain export market share. The cases we reviewed suggest that there are many options for the capital—ranging from self-financing to government guarantees on bank-supplied working capital. And the management talent that's needed to resource an export strategy can also vary. Ultimately, any export strategy is a journey into the unknown, and you can't expect to get the benefits of the success unless you're willing to put resources at risk. If you follow the approach we recommend here, you'll be able to take enough risk to achieve success but won't be betting your company's entire future if your export strategy does not succeed.

Notes

1. Details of the GP Graders case are drawn from Peter Cohan's December 20, 2010 interview with Stuart Payne, and from Export Finance and Insurance Corporation (EFIC), "GP Graders," accessed September 27, 2010, http://www.efic.gov.au/casestudies/Pages/gpgraders.aspx.
2. Details of the Mondavi case are drawn from Murray Silverman, Armand Gilinsky, Jr., Michael Guy, Sally Baack, "Robert Mondavi Corporation," San Francisco State University, June 20, 2001, http://online.sfsu.edu/~castaldi/bie/mondavi.htm.
3. Details of the Footcare case are drawn from "Footcare," EFIC, accessed on September 27, 2010 http://www.efic.gov.au/casestudies/Pages/FootcareInternational.aspx.

Chapter Nine

BRIDGE THE CULTURAL GAP

David St. Thomas was vice president of sales for a mid-size California electronics company. He had built an impressive record over seven years, powering the company from $30 million to just over $200 million—but all within the United States. David was a reasonably aggressive salesman; although not rude or inconsiderate, he was used to getting what he wanted when he wanted it. He had been following leads and cultivating relations in Mexico for some time in the hope of developing some solid interest. Finally he got a definite inquiry from a potential distribution partner.

David hopped a flight to Mexico. When he landed, he went to a restaurant to meet with the head of the distribution company. Always optimistic, he carried a distribution contract in his briefcase that he wanted to get signed so he could hop the next plane back home. That's when David's plan for closing the deal fast ran into a brick wall.

David had flown to Mexico with the intent of signing a contract with his Mexican partner and charging forward to meet his sales targets. But the Mexican partner wanted to spend time dining with the Californian and talking about their families and leisure activities instead of signing the contract or talking business at all.

Looking at this problem through a cultural lens, we can see that the American and the Mexican were in different transactions. The American was selling a product. He was there to book sales. But the Mexican was not so interested in buying a product as he was in establishing a relationship. He felt that other attributes of the transaction also mattered: Is there good personal chemistry? Is there good communication? Is there trust? If there is personal trust and respect, he felt, the odds were good that the transaction would be successful.

The Californian wanted to export the Silicon Valley business culture to Mexico along with his products. That high-tech culture famously focuses on an intense drive to produce ever better financial results, to the exclusion of all else. In contrast, Mexican business culture places a premium on getting to know one's partner in an informal setting before "getting down to business."

Bridging the Cultural Gap as a Key Business Issue

The nub of this chapter's discussion of culture is that you want to feel as comfortable as possible in a foreign setting, and you want your foreign business partner to feel comfortable about you. This requires you to have some degree of familiarity with local culture. You don't need to be a graduate student. You don't need to be an anthropologist. You don't need a deep study of foreign sociology. But you do need to be alert. You do need to be thoughtful. You also need to think about adjustments—possibly just minor ones.

First, a word of definition. By "culture" we do not mean that you need to learn the country's great literary works, their traditional dances, or their exotic cuisine—though it might not hurt to have at least an awareness of these attributes. We are talking about business culture. We think it is important that you understand what's different about how people conduct business in the export market. These differences are not vague or amorphous—they are concrete aspects of day-to-day activity that you take for granted in your home country. Culture is the sea in which we swim. It is the context in which all business—and social—activity takes place. Most people are steeped so thoroughly in their own culture that they sometimes lack awareness of this fact, just as a fish does not notice or question that it is in water.

Understanding cultural differences can help us develop the patience and congeniality necessary to undertake successful business projects. The person without a cultural understanding may look at a foreign development with disdain or fear. The person with an appreciation for culture tends to look at new issues with curiosity and respect. Again, by "culture" we do not mean high culture. We are not trying to encourage foreign business people in Italy to appreciate Italian opera (though there are worse ways to spend an evening). We are suggesting that if you want to do business in Italy, you should be aware of common business and social practices.

This chapter is a little different from the preceding seven chapters, because we are not attempting to comprehensively answer the questions you might encounter concerning culture. It would require an encyclopedia to run through every situation in every country. And business standards tend to evolve as well. For example, the practice of casual dress has taken hold in many countries in the West in the past ten years. So we cannot provide you with hard-and-fast answers in this chapter. What we *can* offer you is a process whereby you can develop your own answers.

First, we delineate attributes of culture that may affect business decision making and everyday life. Second, we describe the global norms for these attributes so you have a reference point as you adjust for local preferences. Third, we leave you with approaches to understanding these cultural differences and how to diagnose your own approach.

Let's begin with attributes of culture. We can group practices in Italy—or anywhere—by certain subjects:

- **Pace of business.** How do you behave when you meet a potential partner or customer for the first time? How do you greet? Can you get right down to business?
- **Gifts.** Should you bring gifts to such meetings? If so, what kind of gift is appropriate?

- **Dress.** What should you wear to such a meeting? Should you err on the side of being overdressed?
- **Punctuality.** Should you arrive five minutes early for your meeting, or is it customary to expect people to arrive twenty minutes late?
- **Friendship.** How to you foster goodwill in a relationship? How do you indicate you value a friendship?
- **Learning.** How do you develop the antennae to understand the differences in the local culture? How do you establish initial rapport?
- **Credibility.** What tests do you need to pass in order for these players to decide to get down to business?
- **Taste.** What are the local preferences in style and taste that might affect business?
- **Details.** How do you master the little things—etiquette, customs, and so on?
- **Traditional societies.** Are there special challenges for women or minorities in business?
- **Caution.** How do you deal with nonstandard business practices such as a request for a bribe or a kickback?

Coming up with the right answer to such cultural issues could make the difference between success and failure. The reason is simple: you will never be able to get down to business in a foreign country unless you can establish a basis of trust. When it comes to establishing trust—and many other business activities—the norms of business culture in the export country are going to be different from the ones in your home country. Proper understanding of the other country's culture sends positive messages to your business partner: *I respect the way you do things. I am comfortable working with you. I hope you are comfortable with me.*

If you want to gain export market share, you will need to identify the most important of these differences and then figure out how to deal with them. We'll help by providing a checklist of tasks you can use to compare your home country with that of the export market. But to make the comparison effectively and learn how and when to adapt, you'll need to enlist the help of the export country's cultural experts.

Key Research Findings on Global Norms

Our research and the case study and advice that follow reveal what may seem obvious: answers to the preceding questions will vary depending on the differences between your home culture and that of the country to which you're seeking to export. Due in part to this variation, there is no one-size-fits-all solution; you will need to develop your own approach that allows you to observe, understand, and adjust. Thus you will not find specific findings here for the previously listed areas of learning, credibility, taste, and details, but general observations appear in the section "How to Adjust to a New Culture."

Here are our findings on the following topics:

1. **Pace of business.** *How do you behave when you meet a potential partner or customer for the first time? How do you greet? Can you get right down to business?* The key point of the meeting is to *establish rapport*. Unless there is trust, respect, and communication, business cannot move ahead. It is useful in initial meetings to try to understand the other party's history and motivations. Each conversation should have a natural flow, and you are wise to take it step by step. Precise advice on pace depends on context, expectations, and the history of discussions. However, do not be afraid to allow a relationship to develop. For example, in many cultures it would be considered inappropriate to discuss business at a meal until the food has been ordered. Initial pleasantries can concern the travel to the country, the hotel, or headlines from the newspaper. In many Asian cultures, business cards should be exchanged with the initial handshake. The recommended pace of business is not likely to be the same in all cases, but you probably should not push to discuss business details over a friendly meal. Depending on the culture, it could take one or more meetings in which *no* business is discussed before

you can reach the level of trust needed to start talking about business. Our key advice: Establish rapport, show interest in the other party's business and life, and proceed incrementally into business matters.

2. **Gifts.** *Should you bring gifts to such meetings? If so, what kind of gift is appropriate?* It is usually appropriate to bring a small ceremonial gift, such as a lacquered box, a coffee-table book, or a decorative paperweight. This is symbolic but shows respect for the meeting. Many companies have specially produced gift items, from golf balls to pens. Our added advice: If the event is at someone's house, it is usually appropriate to bring a hostess-type gift such as candies or flowers.

3. **Dress.** *What should you wear to such a meeting? Should you err on the side of being overdressed?* In general, it is wise to overdress rather than underdress for a meeting. It is appropriate to raise this question with your host: "Do business people normally wear suits to their meetings in this country?" Our advice: Stick with formal business dress for the first meeting unless there is specific guidance to the contrary. Also, it is appropriate to inquire whether there are elements in the schedule that argue for less formal dress, such as a factory or plantation tour.

4. **Punctuality.** *Should you arrive five minutes early for your meeting, or is it customary to expect people to arrive twenty minutes late?* In general, it is better to arrive early even if the person you're meeting is likely to be late. It will certainly put you in a better, more confident mood if you know what the cultural norm is for that country. But you can never help your cause in any culture by keeping the person you're meeting with waiting. Punctuality counts. Our advice: Arrive a few minutes early. (But see a later caution about arriving too early to a Latin American dinner party.)

5. **Friendship.** *How do you foster goodwill in a relationship? How do you indicate you value a friendship?* It certainly helps if you can learn about the person you're going to meet with beforehand. Try to develop bonds outside of the business matters. For example, if you are meeting with the person

who runs a distributor that you'd like to work with in the export country, and you have followed our advice, then you got that person's name from a trusted colleague, such as an accounting firm or law firm partner. If so, you could ask that colleague to tell you about the person's background, interests, and family. Then you can discuss topics likely to be of interest to the person during your initial meeting. Our advice: It makes sense to search for common bonds outside of business.

6. **Traditional Societies.** *Are there special challenges for women or minorities in business?* There can be. Fortunately, we live in an era in which there is a high degree of mobility and success for people regardless of background, but there still can be residual cultural biases at times. This is case-specific. In our experience, if the parties act professionally and with dignity at all times, initial suspicion or hostility is likely to fade. Put a premium on early impressions and a calm, collected professional demeanor. This also means developing the resilience to withstand any potential or perceived slight. Our advice: If you always carry yourself in a professional fashion, the people you deal with will tend to treat you as a professional. Some will come around more quickly than others.

7. **Caution.** *How do you deal with nonstandard business practices such as a request for a bribe or a kickback?* Our advice here is very straightforward: First, be aware of your home country laws. For example, the United States has the Foreign Corrupt Practices Act, which forbids Americans from bribing foreigners. Other countries have similar acts. Second, be aware of host country laws. What is considered a gift and what is considered a bribe? Third, most companies additionally have their own rules as to what might be an appropriate gift between business partners. You need to be able to cite this language if you are asked for a bribe or to otherwise be party to an illegal activity.

How to Adjust to a New Culture

Now that you have a reference point as to the global norms for business transactions between different cultures, you can adjust these norms to your particular situation. Each country has its particular cultural norms that differ from those of other countries, and there can be additional intracountry differences depending on local culture, socioeconomic status, ethnicity, language, and so on. As we mentioned before, this chapter does not provide an encyclopedic response. Better to provide an approach that will serve you well regardless of the country you visit.

By following these tips, you can develop your awareness and understanding of local culture. Over time, through a series of successful interactions, you will gain credibility. The people you interact with in the export market will take note of your sensitivity and good judgment in dealing with the "small stuff"—and thus perceive you as likely to show the same sensitivity and judgment when it comes to the "big stuff."

1. **Arrive a day early and observe.** Walk around town and observe how people interact with each other. For example, do men hold doors or pull out chairs for women? Are smoking and drinking common at meal times? What time do people arrive at work and when do they leave? Consider having a meal in a nicer business restaurant and discreetly observing behavior. How do business colleagues greet—with a handshake, a hug, a quick peck, or a slap on the back?

2. **Get expert advice.** Undertake courtesy calls with the local branch of your bank, your accounting firm, and your law firm. On the one hand, you are honestly trying to gain local knowledge. On the other hand, you are trying to take business meetings with friendly parties where there is no real business at stake. This is your dress rehearsal. You can typically open up the discussion. So at the end of the visit with the accountant, you can simply say, "A major customer has invited me to his home for dinner tonight. Could you please advise me what would be considered a proper gift to bring on such an occasion?" We also advise you to ask the same question of different experts in the hope of finding a convergent answer. The concierge at the hotel and the maître d' at the restaurant will also have good advice on hospitality, etiquette, and other norms.

3. **Listen and learn.** Go to a chamber of commerce luncheon. If you are a member of a civic organization like Kiwanis, Rotary, or Young Presidents' Organization (YPO), attend a local function. See whether your college has an alumni chapter in town. Read a version of the local newspaper in your language the day you'll be meeting with your contact so you can be familiar with what is happening in the country and what is likely to be of concern to your host when you meet.
4. **Don't fake it.** Your hosts know you are a foreigner. You don't have to pretend you are a local. If you are an American visiting Mexico for the first time, or if you are an Australian visiting Indonesia for the first time, it is OK to freely admit this. Your hosts are not expecting someone with deep knowledge of Mexico or Indonesia. They are expecting someone who can work within their business practices and who treats them with respect and friendship.

Bridging the Cultural Gap: A Case Study

We examine the challenge of bridging the cultural gap by looking at the case of **Electrolux/Zanussi**, a Swedish appliance maker, which initially ran into trouble when workers at the Italian appliance maker it acquired viewed Electrolux as "Vikings from the North." Then we offer **basics of business interactions across cultures,** covering some common differences in the way people in different cultures perform the daily rituals of business interaction.

Electrolux/Zanussi

Imagine that you head a company that's been very successful in a part of the world that shares a common culture, and you decide that in order to grow you'll need to move into a very different part of the world. To get there, you decide to buy a struggling company in that

(Continued)

206 EXPORT NOW: FIVE KEYS TO ENTERING NEW MARKETS

Electrolux/Zanussi (Continued)

country. You then run into a buzz saw of resistance from the struggling company's employees, who are reluctant to be managed by what they perceive as foreign invaders.

This, in essence, is the cultural conflict that surfaced with the 1984 merger of Sweden's Electrolux, a global home appliance maker, and Zanussi, a thirty-thousand-employee Italian manufacturer of refrigerators, washing machines, and cookers. This deal took years to integrate, and as a result, shareholders, customers, and employees suffered. Electrolux bent over backward to counter the perception—developed by Zanussi's powerful employee union before the merger closed—that Electrolux was invading their company as "Vikings from the North." To change that perception, Electrolux worked long and hard with key Zanussi stakeholders to be very sensitive about issues such as cost cutting.[1]

Electrolux plowed forward, despite the resistance, and agreed to maintain all Zanussi's important functions in Italy. This meant that Electrolux agreed to keep the level of employment in Italy the same after the deal closed—even though Electrolux realized that if it did this, unfortunately, the business would be unprofitable.

The cultural differences created many internal problems that put the company at a disadvantage relative to aggressive competitors. Zanussi lost market share in Italy. A plant automation project that would have made the company more competitive was delayed because workers there were afraid of it. And support for the deal among 150 Zanussi middle managers evaporated over time.

Despite these problems, Electrolux's management of the cultural differences enabled it to boost Zanussi's financial results from a loss of 120 billion Italian lire in 1984 to a 60-billion lire profit in 1987. This outcome was partly a result of cost cutting but also due to effective teamwork between Electrolux and Zanussi. The cost-cutting steps included a 4,848-employee headcount reduction, increased Zanussi sourcing from Electrolux that led to a 2-percent saving on purchases, and improved production technology. On the softer side, Electrolux's management of the merger integration convinced sixty managers at Zanussi to support the merger, thanks to harmony-promoting steps such as creating a new board, forming integration task forces, creating a new culture and organization, and spurring innovation.

Although the challenges of managing cultural differences in a merger are different from those you'll face as you take your business into export markets, the Electrolux/Zanussi case can offer three useful lessons:

- **Don't assume that you will be welcomed with open arms.** When you initially suggest the idea of working together, make sure that you anticipate differences. If you do, then you won't be surprised when approaches that work in your home country backfire in the export market.
- **Be prepared to adapt your cultural approach to the export market.** Electrolux had traditionally been very aggressive about achieving efficiencies after it completed an acquisition. However, once it decided to invest in Zanussi, it needed to adapt the way it approached setting and achieving goals for its Italian subsidiary. Electrolux demonstrated an amazing ability to work with its Italian colleagues without losing sight of its efforts to boost profitability. Such willingness to adapt working style while keeping in mind financial goals is a hallmark of successful bridging of the cultural gap.
- **Create a shared governance model.** To bridge the cultural gap, it is essential that you agree with your partner

(Continued)

Electrolux/Zanussi (*Continued*)

on a way of governing the alliance. Such agreements should create a joint operating committee—consisting of executives from your company and your partner's—that sets goals, develops strategy, and directs both organizations to take the steps needed to implement the strategy.

Basics of Business Interactions Across Cultures

There are many ways in which differences in culture can affect how you need to operate in an export market. If you sell a consumer product, you need to know people's eating habits in the export country and how they differ from those in your home country. Moreover, the kinds of people you sell your product to in your home market may be very different from the ones who will buy it in the export market. Here are some examples of how people perform basic business activities in different countries:[2]

1. **How to greet in different regions.** If the people you're meeting are men, then it is always acceptable to shake hands on meeting. In China, you might initiate a gentle handshake or make a short bow from the shoulders. In Japan, the bow comes from the waist, and the lower the bow, the more you're signaling respect to your colleague. In Latin America and Europe, proper business greeting etiquette consists of a firm handshake, a smile, and direct eye contact. In the Middle East and Asia, offer a gentle handshake and a greeting. In Arab countries, never shake hands with your left hand, which is considered unclean.

2. **Who to greet first by culture.** In some cultures you should greet the oldest person in a group first; in others, the first person introduced is the one at the top of the business hierarchy. Be formal when addressing someone—using formal titles such as Doctor, Mister, Director, or Engineer is a safe

approach. In Europe and the Americas, handshakes between men and women are common. In some instances a man will merely greet a woman, with handshakes only if the woman extends her hand first.

3. **Dress codes for men and women.** Men will be safe wearing a conservative business suit with darker colors, formal tie, and jacket. In Argentina, for example, being well-dressed boosts the level of respect and professionalism you can expect from others. Women should choose conventional business clothing; long sleeves, skirts below the knee, and modest necklines are a must. In Latin America, Europe, and the United States, a well-cut suit will be appropriate for women—particularly in more conservative countries.

4. **Table manners in different countries.** Table manners can affect a business relationship. In Arab countries the left hand is considered unclean, so don't eat with it. In Latin America, a dinner party guest should arrive between ten and twenty minutes after the official start time; the guest who arrives too soon may be seen as greedy. In Japan there may be a strict protocol for the order in which food is eaten, and chopsticks are often used. And in China, slurping and speaking with your mouth full is acceptable. In some countries, loud burping is considered a way to show your appreciation of the food.

How to Not Step on a Landmine

Before we close this discussion of culture, we also want to review the "Nos" and cautionary points that can trip up business people in a foreign culture.

First, be cautious about humor. Different societies appreciate some kinds of humor and frown on others or even take offense. To be on the safe side, avoid sexually explicit humor. And humor based on sarcasm or irony often does not translate easily. Our advice is to avoid trying to tell your favorite joke to your host until you have developed a sense of what works and what does not.

Second, be wary of making negative comments. Sounds obvious enough, but in poorer countries visitors can be quite harsh in their assessment, without attempting to be critical. So if your host asks you how your hotel was, avoid stating "It was a dump." Americans may have a low opinion (or no opinion) of cricket as a sport, but they should refrain from passing on those views to local enthusiasts. And cricket fans should avoid disparaging comments about baseball. Even comments that would be considered casual in your home country, such as "I can't believe how slowly traffic is moving" or "Is the pollution always this bad?" could be considered a deliberate insult in a foreign country. As you get to know the individual, you can also develop a sense of how thin-skinned—or tolerant—he may be.

Third, be wary of sensitive topics. Avoid politics and religious comments until you have established a high degree of familiarity with individuals. In western countries it is quite common for people to make offhand critical comments about political leaders or even to ridicule them. In many other countries this is considered a serious insult.

Fourth, don't take offense and don't escalate. You may need to develop a thick skin yourself occasionally. Locals may comment on developments they have heard about in your country, even if these events are unusual or the truth is stretched a bit. You need to be able to weather such comments and unusual questions in good humor. We might consider some questions to be ill-advised or in questionable taste, but you should try to engage in an upbeat, nondefensive fashion. Regardless of which country you are from, a cab driver might ask, "So why does your country always try to boss us around?" or more pointedly, "Why does your country always start wars?" Your best weapon here is a smile and a disarming quip: "I think the only people I have ever tried to boss around are my kids, and it never seems to work." If the other person really is trying to provoke you, it is important you retain your composure and your smile: "I'm afraid you will have to put that question to our foreign ministry; I am simply a businessman."

Lessons for the Silicon Valley Executive in Mexico

What happened to David St. Thomas, the electronics VP of sales? The result of the mismatched cultures was that the Californian lost patience with his Mexican partner and gave up on his efforts to build a business in Mexico.

This case reveals some important lessons. Different people and different cultures have different approaches to business activity. We can say the American was "wrong" only insofar as he was unaware of or insensitive to his customers' cultural norms. There is an old saying from politics that sums this up: "People don't care what you know until they know that you care." In other words, the Mexican did not want to talk about a transaction until he was comfortable in the relationship. In many countries around the world a party who is far removed from the parent company will naturally prefer to seek personal connectivity.

Bridging the Cultural Gap Checklist

Have you really figured out how to bridge the cultural gap? To answer that question in the affirmative, you should have specific answers to each of the following questions.

Questions
Visit the local bank to exchange currency. Are people dressed formally or casually? Are people addressed as "Mister," "Ma'am," or local equivalents?
What term of address do clerks and shopkeepers use with customers?
Go to a business restaurant and note how people greet. Do they shake hands? Bow? Peck on the cheek? Do they exchange business cards? Do people regularly toast with alcoholic beverages?
Who can you ask what time normal office hours start and end?
How can you determine when local holidays occur and a brief summary of the holiday?
Are you well-versed in your country's laws and those of the export country regarding nonstandard practices?

Conclusion

Many people who travel abroad at first become aware of the perceived shortcomings of the new countries. They cannot get their favorite television show. They cannot find their favorite breakfast cereal. The telephones are different. The ATM does not work the same way. Everything is a bit off. A bit confusing. A bit frustrating. To a certain extent, some of this reaction is normal. And foreigners may feel very much the same when they visit *your* country.

Our hope is that, as you develop the navigational skills to use the phones and the maps locally, you also begin to realize that, regardless of the specific country, your new market has many strengths and successful attributes as well. And we hope you also start to realize that regardless of what society you are in, businesspeople around the world have much in common. Your ability to work with people from different countries—people from different cultures—will serve you well as you develop a global business.

Notes

1. Dag Andersson et al., "Electrolux: The Acquisition and Integration of Zanussi," *INSEAD-CEDEP*, 1989.
2. "Business Etiquette While Traveling," *TravelEtiquette*, accessed October 27, 2010, http://www.traveletiquette.co.uk/business-etiquette-when-travelling.html.

Chapter Ten

TAKE ACTION

The first nine chapters have prepared you for this moment—
taking action. Up to this point, here's what we've advised
you to do:

- Look at the world outside your company and see if you can
find a way to take advantage of global growth (Chapter One).
- Look inside to determine whether your company has the desire
and discipline needed to seize those growth opportunities
(Chapter Two).
- Pick an export country that is most likely to lead to a successful
outcome (Chapter Three).
- Understand potential customers in the export market to discern
how to find them and what makes them different from the
ones you're used to (Chapter Four).
- Analyze the competition you'll face in the export market
and decide whether your company can find a niche in that
competitive ecosystem (Chapter Five).
- Figure out what capabilities you'll need—whether they be
distribution, warehousing, manufacturing, or regulatory skills—
to win export market share (Chapter Six).
- Pick an export market partner to gain the additional skills
you need to win (Chapter Seven).
- Acquire both the capital and the management time you need
to get your export strategy off the ground and keep it moving
(Chapter Eight).

- Educate yourself on the cultural differences between your home country and the export market and adapt accordingly (Chapter Nine).

Key Lessons

We think these chapters suggest an important mental model that should guide you as you leap into the tumultuous waters of exporting:

- Move incrementally.
- Experiment and test markets.
- Become a learning organization.
- Develop a feedback mechanism so you can tell when you are going the wrong way.
- Be willing to adjust.

Now that you've done all that research, you are better prepared to take action. And that is what we urge you to do now. Here's our advice on what to do next—arrayed in order from the least complicated to the most complicated.

Learn

- **Visit the export promotion agency** in your country to learn who can help you in the export market and to become familiar with some of the basics of exporting there. The U.S. Department of Commerce's Gold Key Program (see table) is a good example.
- **Find out who the big customers and competitors are** in the export market.
- **Get smart about exporting** by reading books on the topic and attending lectures at local colleges.
- **Attend presentations** at your local chamber of commerce.
- **Identify bilateral business organizations** (for example, the German-American Business Association, the Australia-Indonesia Business Council).
- **Explore what information your domestic industry association or trade association has** to offer about overseas markets.

Many associations have overseas affiliate members that can be a source of information.

U.S. Department of Commerce Gold Key Matching Service

Many countries offer export promotion support for businesses. One of the stronger such programs is the U.S. Department of Commerce Gold Key program, but we encourage you to visit with your country's export promotion agency.

The U.S. Commercial Service can help you find potential overseas agents, distributors, sales representatives, and business partners.

Gold Key Matching Service Benefits

- Reduce the time and money you invest in locating and screening prospective trade partners.
- Spend your time doing what you do best—managing your company. Let the U.S. Commercial Service arrange business meetings with prescreened contacts, representatives, distributors, professional associations, government contacts, and/or licensing or joint venture partners.

Gold Key Matching Service Features

- Customized market and industry briefings with trade specialists.
- Timely and relevant market research.
- Appointments with prospective trade partners in key industry sectors.
- Post-meeting debriefing with trade specialists and assistance in developing appropriate follow-up strategies.

(Continued)

> - Help with travel, accommodations, interpreter service, and clerical support.
> - If your schedule or travel budget limits your ability to travel overseas, consider Video Services. You can receive all the benefits of the Gold Key Matching Services, but meet your potential business partners via videoconferencing instead of in person.
>
> *Source:* export.gov.[1]

Connect

- **Follow your customers overseas.** If your big customers are going into a new country, talk with them about how you can help them in those new markets. Meet with your customer's country head in the new market.
- **Set up your company's web site so that it can take orders from foreign customers.** To do that you'll need to translate it into the right language(s) and enable payment mechanisms that work there. Check your web page fields for phone number and mail code flexibility to ensure that foreign residents can easily use your web pages. Can you be located by foreign language search engines?

Go

- **Attend international trade fairs for your industry.** Such attendance might cost you $1,000. It can give you very helpful connections, market leads, insight into what competitors are doing, and a sense of how much opportunity you might have in the export market.
- **Go on a trade mission sponsored by your country's export promotion organization.** Such missions might cost you between $5,000 and $10,000. They are a way to get introductions to key decision makers in the export market, including government officials and corporate leaders.
- **Put together your own trade mission, meaning plan your own trip to promote exports.** For this you will probably spend

the most. You will be making a visit to the export market that is specifically tailored to your company's needs. Before going, you should arrange to meet with banks, industry associations, lawyers, accountants, and your country's local export promotion officer in the export market.

We urge you to get started. Don't feel you must wait until you have perfect information before doing anything. It's better to do something with good information; once you have done it, you'll learn and can adjust your strategy based on that learning.

A Final Word: Share

Thank you for letting us share with you some of the lessons we have learned over years of working with companies around the world. We hope you will also be able to share your lessons with us.

Exporting your company's product is an exciting way for your business to grow. Along with this book, we are writing a blog; we invite you to visit www.exportnow.com and share your stories about your export efforts. We want to build a community of like-minded people who can share their experiences and help you avoid some of the pitfalls of exporting while seizing the opportunities.

So keep in touch with us, and we will keep pushing forward to give you the best information and advice we can find about how your company can reach its export market share goals.

Please let us know what you liked about the book, as well as places where we need to do a better job. We want to hear what worked and what didn't work.

And we want to hear good news about your company's efforts.

Happy exporting!

Frank Lavin
Peter Cohan
Email: frank@exportnow.com
Email: peter@exportnow.com
Blog: ExportNow.com

Note

1. "The Gold Key Matching Service," Export.gov, accessed November 7, 2010, http://www.export.gov/salesandmarketing/eg_main_018195. asp.

INDEX